The
DEALMAKER

The
DEALMAKER

HOW TO SUCCEED
IN BUSINESS & LIFE
THROUGH DEDICATION,
DETERMINATION & DISRUPTION

MAURICIO UMANSKY
with EMILY LIEBERT

G

GALLERY BOOKS

NEW YORK   LONDON   TORONTO   SYDNEY   NEW DELHI

G⫯

Gallery Books
An Imprint of Simon & Schuster, Inc.
1230 Avenue of the Americas
New York, NY 10020

First Gallery Books hardcover edition April 2023

GALLERY BOOKS and colophon are registered trademarks
of Simon & Schuster, Inc.

For information about special discounts for bulk purchases, please
contact Simon & Schuster Special Sales at 1-866-506-1949 or
business@simonandschuster.com.

The Simon & Schuster Speakers Bureau can bring authors to your live event. For
more information or to book an event, contact the Simon & Schuster Speakers
Bureau at 1-866-248-3049 or visit our website at www.simonspeakers.com.

Interior design by Jaime Putorti

Manufactured in the United States of America

10 9 8 7 6 5 4 3 2 1

Library of Congress Cataloging-in-Publication Data

Names: Umansky, Mauricio, author. | Liebert, Emily, author.
Title: The dealmaker : how to succeed in business and life through dedication,
    determination and disruption / Mauricio Umansky, with Emily Liebert.
Description: New York : Gallery Books, [2023]
Identifiers: LCCN 2022061494 (print) | LCCN 2022061495 (ebook) |
    ISBN 9781668010648 (hardcover) | ISBN 9781668010662 (ebook)
Subjects: LCSH: Success in business. | Success. | Businesspeople—United
    States. | Real estate business—United States.
Classification: LCC HF5386 .U36 2023 (print) | LCC HF5386 (ebook) |
    DDC 650.1—dc23/eng/20230104
LC record available at https://lccn.loc.gov/2022061494
LC ebook record available at https://lccn.loc.gov/2022061495

ISBN 978-1-6680-1064-8
ISBN 978-1-6680-1066-2 (ebook)

Dedicated to my family, clients, and colleagues for the trust and support that has carried me through the years

CONTENTS

CONTENTS

The DEALMAKER

INTRODUCTION

How was your day?" My wife, Kyle, asked, greeting me at the front door with a welcoming smile and already anticipating my typical answer.

"It was amazing. The best day of my life," I replied, kissing her on the lips.

She laughed. "How is it possible that every single day is that perfect for you?"

"When you're passionate about what you do and you love the people and the place you come home to, that's just the way it is."

It was the only explanation I could offer, and I knew it to be true, especially because we were in the trenches of launching a business from the ground up and it was a wild roller-coaster ride, fraught with rapid inclines, sharp turns, and steep slopes.

There was rarely a reprieve from the chaos. We'd set up shop with three days' notice and were clamoring to get everything done. Plastic rentals served as our desk chairs; our transaction coordinator doubled as the receptionist; my partner Billy Rose was making runs to the Home Depot to swap out the dilapidated toilet seats, and our office had such horrific parking that I was acting as the valet. If our agents needed to leave, I would literally run downstairs and move cars so that they could arrive at their listings on time. We were a small team but a motivated one. We rolled up our sleeves. Got our hands dirty. And made shit happen.

"Most people would be exhausted and overwhelmed in your position." Kyle shook her head incredulously. "I don't know how you do it all and remain so positive."

She was right. Most people would have been completely stressed out in my shoes. But I'm not most people, and learning to find balance in my life, while maintaining an optimistic outlook, is something that was ingrained in me from a young age.

As a child, my grandfather Abraham taught me this important historical adage: "There are twenty-four hours in a day—eight for sleep, eight for work, and eight for play. It's up to you to decide how to divide your time wisely." I've carried this advice with me for the last five decades, as I've strived to give 100 percent to everything I do, which includes my career, my personal relationships, and the many extracurricular activities that fulfill me.

Striking this balance is often easier said than done, yet I believe that if you lead with confidence and a positive attitude, success is not only achievable but probable, and the possibilities are endless.

This way of thinking originates from my upbringing and being raised by a very loving and supportive Jewish family from the day I was born on June 25, 1970, in Mexico City. Judaism was a big part of my life growing up. Even though we weren't orthodox, we honored holidays and traditions—imparted by my mother—which I still follow today. My grandparents emigrated, by boat, from Russia, Lithuania, Turkey, and Minsk—fleeing these countries, as so many Jews did in order to obtain freedom—and landed in Mexico, where my parents were born, so I was a second-generation Mexican.

My parents; my sister, Sharon; and I ate dinner together every night, and my father, who's always had a passion for philosophical books, would talk to us about Dostoevsky and all kinds of existential stuff. So, early on, we were part of these very interesting and educational conversations that taught us we could do anything we put our minds to. The world was our oyster.

But well before I became one of the top ten real estate agents in the country, boasting the most homes sold above twenty million dollars, I had quite a bit to overcome. The first major obstacle I faced was being born with a potentially fatal blood disease called neutropenia, which is when you have too few neutrophils, a type of white blood cell that fights infection and bacteria. At the time I was diagnosed with neutropenia, most people died from it. Therefore, the first six years of my life were consumed by my parents' fear.

I was their first child and the first grandchild in the family, which meant I grew up extremely nurtured and bolstered, particularly since I had this horrible disease and was at the hospital multiple times a week, if not every day, being poked and prodded and having my blood taken. I basically got away with whatever I wanted because my family didn't want to upset me.

Incredibly, when I was six years old, after a visit to the Boston Children's Hospital for a regular blood test, the doctors told me I was cured and that I no longer had neutropenia. It was a medical miracle that set the tone for the self-assured man I was destined to become.

Still, the trauma of those six years took a mental toll on me and are completely blocked from my memory.

It was at this point that my family decided we needed a fresh start, and we relocated from Mexico to Bel Air, a residential neighborhood in Los Angeles, California. We moved there for a few reasons. One was that there was a major devaluation of the peso in addition to other politically motivated concerns in Mexico. Another was so my father could diversify the family textile business he was running with his two brothers and my grandfather. They knew better than to put all of their eggs in one basket, and my father volunteered to pursue opportunities in America—a resolution that allowed my mother to follow her dream of becoming a psychologist. Ultimately, she received her MFCC license, her doctorate, and two postdoctoral degrees in psychology, which had a major impact on me as a young man. I learned through her, innately, an understanding of the human brain, human behavior, and psychology. She taught me how to read people, a skill that led me to become the strong salesman I am today.

But, my impediments didn't end in our new home. As a result of the constant attention to my neutropenia, it somehow went undiagnosed—until I was about nine years old—that I was legally blind in one eye. I remember the moment I found out like it was yesterday. My mother took me to the pediatrician for my annual checkup, and they tested my eyesight by having me put a piece of paper over each eye while I read the letter chart with the other eye (there were no fancy machines back then!). It wasn't the first time I'd done this, but, unknowingly, I'd always managed to cheat the system by moving my head to one side so I could see with my good eye. But this time, the woman doing the test told me to keep still. All of a sudden, I realized I couldn't see a thing with my bad eye. It was completely shocking, not only to me but to my parents too.

What was so astonishing is that my blind eye had never hindered me. From the time I was two years old, I was the most athletic kid around. I could hit the baseball farther than anyone I knew, and I excelled in every sport I tried. There was no reason for anyone to suspect that I could see only 50 percent as well as everyone else.

You'd think I would have listened to the doctor and used the patch she instructed me to wear, in an attempt to

strengthen my blind eye, which would have been a possibility if I'd followed the rules. But I was having none of it.
I would remove the patch when I went to school and at any
chance I got. Eventually, my mother realized that things were
not improving and that tough love was the only answer. She
took me to the park that afternoon, put patches on both of my
eyes, and instructed me to run around and play, which was
obviously impossible. I was crying so hard because I couldn't
see at all. Her response to my hysterics was "Do you want to
be partially blind for the rest of your life? Wear the patch,
Mauricio."

Remarkably, I still didn't heed this advice, and my vision
remains 20/400 in one eye. Fortunately, as with every other
hindrance I've encountered throughout my life, I've found a
way to thrive in spite of it.

This includes the academically encumbering ADD I've also
endured since I was a young child, which made sitting in a classroom and completing homework assignments especially taxing
for me. Because of this, I was not an exemplary student, even
though I was very smart and able to absorb all the material. I
would score well on exams but then fail to turn in my assignments,
much to the frustration of my parents, who didn't understand why
I couldn't get it done and had to force me to do so in order to help
me move on to the next grade level, which was always a relief!

The fact is, I didn't care about how I did in school. The only
thing that mattered to me was my athletic endeavors. That was

where my drive and ambition were centered—I was a competitive guy through and through, and I needed to win. (I'm still that way!) Whether it was soccer, football, tennis, racquetball, or any other activity, I would always beat my friends, even if I was down on my knees while they were on their feet, or if I was holding the Ping-Pong paddle with my nondominant hand while they played with their dominant hands.

In high school, I ended up turning my focus to snow skiing in a serious way. I wanted to become an Olympic skier, and my parents supported that. In fact, in 1986, I created the Mexican Olympic ski team. While we didn't compete in the 1988 Olympics in Calgary, we did pave the way for the next generation to finally send a Mexican Olympic ski team to Albertville in 1992.

With this accomplishment under my belt, I decided to return to Mexico for my senior year. I'd been at a small, private Jewish school through junior high and had transferred to a public school with a better athletic program for part of high school, but it was not a good fit for me. So I went to live with my cousin Sammy's family in Mexico—Sammy is my age and has been my best friend all my life. He was the one who suggested that we do our senior year together at the American School Foundation in Mexico City and my parents gave me their blessing.

By some miracle I ended up graduating, though not exactly on time. I walked in the ceremony, but I did fail algebra my senior year, so I had to go to summer school at

Beverly Hills High School in order to finish. After struggling through that, I knew I needed to take a beat before applying to college.

In light of this, Sammy and I embarked on a one-year sabbatical through Europe and Israel. Our fathers gave us each five thousand dollars and said, "Come back when the money runs out," which was about thirteen months later. We stayed in three different kibbutz communities in Israel for about seven months. Then from there, we backpacked through Egypt and Europe for another six months. We slept in hostels and on trains; I'll never forget one specific "hotel," where the rooms were two dollars a night. A far cry from the suites I stay in now!

Regardless, it was the experience of a lifetime, which went a long way in developing my street smarts, as we were forced to communicate and negotiate in languages that were foreign to us. Seeing the world like that and absorbing the history made a lasting impression on me. Even though I was never a good student, I can still quote Leonardo da Vinci, Michelangelo, and Napoléon Bonaparte, which proves that just because you don't excel academically doesn't mean you're unintelligent or that you can't possess a thirst for knowledge.

Along these lines, upon our return, I ended up enrolling in Santa Monica College, which was a junior community college, where I remained for two years. I still had no idea what I wanted to do career-wise and was much more interested in going surfing in the morning and skiing in the afternoon. Yet it was the first time I actually enjoyed learning in a formal capacity, because I was able to take classes that appealed to me, such as business law, accounting, and economics, and this allowed me to get excited about a vocation outside of athletics.

After two years of college, all of my friends still had two years left to go, and I was at a crossroads. I could either continue my education at a four-year school or go directly into the workforce. This timing happened to coincide with a major recession, and my dad called me up and said, "Listen, I'm kind of sick of taking care of you while you're bumming around and, now with the current financial challenges, it's not the same world it was before. You need to either get a job or go to school, but I'm no longer supporting you being a pseudo athlete or just having fun."

I knew he was right. And since my parents had supported me in every way possible throughout my entire life, instilling me with the confidence that—despite the obstacles I'd had— I could achieve anything I wanted, I chose to forego any further schooling and join my father's textile company, which my grandfather had started and I planned to take over one day. It was one of the best decisions I've ever made.

The moral here is that you have to do what's best for you and for your future. And if you're lucky, as I was, your family will encourage you to follow your passion. I carry this belief with me to this day. Without question, my wife, Kyle, and I have always provided our four daughters with copious amounts of confidence and love. We want them to feel like they can do anything and that they *deserve* to do anything. You want to become president of the United States? You absolutely have the ability to make that happen.

Being raised with this level of devotion was an invaluable gift my parents bestowed upon me, and I've passed this gift along to my own children. Just knowing that the sky is the limit has allowed me to continue to grow and prosper in ways I never imagined I would, and I want the same for them.

It's mantras like this one, which span my fifty-two years of life, my thirty-plus years as a businessman, and my twenty-seven years as a husband and father that will fill the pages of this book. It's part memoir and part career and leadership manifesto, and my hope is that it will inspire aspiring entrepreneurs and self-starters across all industries. My objective is to embolden those who are ready to work hard and are prepared to meet adversity head-on, which I've done and still do every day. Success doesn't materialize overnight. It requires endless stamina, grit, and dedication, and I will share what it takes to achieve everything you want and then some.

I've experienced a lot of highs and lows, both professionally and personally, to get where I am today as founder and CEO of The Agency—an industry-disrupting real estate firm. Since we launched in 2011, The Agency has ranked among the

Inc. 5000 list of the fastest-growing private companies in the country for five consecutive years, and we've grown to employ nearly 1,500 agents across seventy offices in eight countries. I've represented some of the world's most significant properties, including the Playboy Mansion, the first house in LA to sell over the $100 million mark, the Walt Disney estate, and residences owned by Michael Jackson, Michael Jordan, and Prince. But these achievements haven't come to me through luck or without stumbling blocks along the way.

I'll take you through what it was like to join my father's business, start my own fashion brands, work for—and ultimately part ways with—my brother-in-law Rick Hilton's company, get fired during a recession, find my career passion, and launch The Agency. Each chapter will center around a specific piece of wisdom I've learned, and I'll expand on the insights gleaned from those takeaways.

Of course life isn't only about business. This book is also about flourishing in my personal life. I'll talk about what it means to be a loyal husband and an attentive father and discuss the challenges of maintaining a solid, twenty-seven-year marriage while trying to be a present and loving dad, as I also worked tirelessly to build my career.

Last but definitely not least, I'll reveal my fundamental principles for those who are determined to chase their dreams, achieve success in business and life, and improve their overall well-being.

If there's one thing I can say for sure, it's that when one door closes, another door opens. You have the ability to create opportunities for yourself and make lemonade out of even the most sour lemons. This is something I focus on every single day, and I hope you will too.

CHAPTER 1

PLAY HARD, WORK HARDER

A dream doesn't become reality through magic; it
takes sweat, determination and hard work.
—Colin Powell, sixty-fifth US secretary of state

Building on my grandfather's sage advice to find balance in life—eight hours for sleep, eight hours for work, and eight hours for play—my decision to leave college after two years and join my father's textile company felt right. School just wasn't for me, but once I'd taken various business classes, it became clear to me that pursuing a career in sales was my calling. Given my outgoing personality and my ability to understand people, I knew it would be something I was good at. The big question was: What was my path going to look like? I thought the best way to answer that and to get my feet wet was by working for my father and learning everything I could from his vast experience.

THE VALUE OF A PENNY

One of the first things my father taught me was the importance of margins and that every cent, as opposed to every dollar, counts. This may sound like a deliberate exaggeration, especially when you're thinking in terms of real estate sales in the millions, but in the textile industry, a penny—or even a fraction of a penny—can make a big difference in profitability.

I'll never forget selling piece goods for roughly ninety-six cents and my dad telling me I had to battle to add two more cents to the price. I would explain to him that the buyer was tough and that I'd already negotiated.

I'd ask, "Why are you making me go back to him for a couple of cents?"

And he'd sit across the desk from me and do the math. Then he'd say, "Come back to me when you have a deal for ninety-eight cents."

Two cents! It sounds crazy, right? Well, think of it this way . . . let's pretend I was selling 150,000 yards of fabric, multiplied by two cents. That's three thousand more in profit for one order. When you consider the fact that we were selling two million yards a month, which is two million yards times twelve months times two cents, all of a sudden we're talking about $480,000. And if you can somehow up that two cents to five cents, you're bringing in $1.2 million extra annually. Translation: My father was completely justified in pushing me to fight for the increase, as insignificant as it may have sounded to me.

Today, I use this same lesson, but I apply it to real estate. I teach all of my agents that lowering their commission by 1 percent, or even half a percent, in order to give the seller or buyer more money and, therefore, get a deal done may not seem like a major concession, but it can amount to big money for our firm in the long run. Check this out—let's say a successful agent brings in $40 million a year in sales, which—with a 6 percent commission—means they make $2.4 million. If they lower their commission to 5 percent, suddenly they're only making $2 million, which is a major loss, especially if you start multiplying that by all the agents who work for us. For this reason, I instill in them my father's method of doing things—which is to negotiate for every decimal point. There's no reason to drop from 6 percent to 5 percent immediately. Even half a decimal point could be the difference in millions of dollars, and that money goes directly to our bottom line. It has zero expenses attached to it.

Understanding value from that perspective is a message I've carried with me in all aspects of my professional life.

A SALESMAN IS BORN

Of course there's a lot more that goes into becoming a great salesperson than margins. One of those things is figuring out how to bring in new accounts and, also, handling accounts that are challenging. My father was not someone who believed in nepotism and—now that two of my daughters work for me—neither am I. My dad always gave me the toughest accounts and had me running all over Los Angeles to drum up new deals so I could help him grow the business. If you don't have to roll up your sleeves and get your hands dirty, you're not going to appreciate the "high of the sale" when you do achieve your goal. I remember how amazing that adrenaline rush felt in the very beginning. I'd get in my car after landing an order, turn up the music, and dance! It became an addiction for me, and I couldn't stop. I still feel that way to this day.

I believe that if you're a strong and motivated salesperson you can sell anything, because selling is not about the product. It's easy to study and amass knowledge about whatever product you're selling. But, in order to really succeed as a salesperson, you need to:

- *Read the room.* This in essence means read the people. What are they looking for? What are their goals? Their needs and wants? What kind of energy do they have?

• *Don't rest on your laurels.* Continue to deliver excellent service, even once the deal is done. You can't fall off after that, because real estate is a relationship-based business, and you're only as good as your last sale. The moment that contract is complete, the client is free to work with another agent, which is not what you want. So it's very important to let your client know that you care by staying in touch with them. That's how you win their business back the next time they're looking to buy or sell a home and, also, how you receive referrals from them in the meantime.

• *Be a chameleon.* Understand how to communicate in various circumstances. It's critical that the person who's buying from you is able to trust you and believe that you're knowledgeable about the product you're selling. For example, if it's fabric, you want to know if it's going to shrink. And, if so, how much is it going to shrink? Or will it stretch out? And how much is it going to stretch? Is the color going to bleed? It's essential to be prepared to answer every question you can think of.

• *Listen.* Sometimes you literally need to close your mouth and stop yourself from speaking. Clients want to feel heard. Often they need to feel heard in order to move forward. Many salespeople don't get this, and because of that, they're unable to read the room, which always ends up backfiring.

• *Love what you're selling.* If this doesn't come naturally in your chosen field, you have to find some aspect of it that drives you—beyond the financial return. So, while real estate is my ultimate passion, when I was in the textile industry, my mind was solely focused on that, which made me fall in love with it. And, I promise you, the textile industry is tough. My clients would scream at me regularly, specifically when there were crazy deadlines to be met, which there always were . . . which leads me to my next point.

• *Take things in stride.* Even at twenty-two years old, when I was being yelled at by maniacal fifty-year-old men about delays in the textile business, I didn't let it bother me. I would allow them to vent, and when they got tired of ranting, I'd respond calmly and close the deal.

Clearly, over the course of my career, I've learned a lot more about sales, but this was an eye-opening start for me and, in many respects, it only got easier from there.

TIME IS MONEY

It sounds so simple, right? And you hear people throw this expression around casually, which—in its most basic form—means when you waste time, it can be costly. When you're in sales, this saying denotes how productive or unproductive you are. For example, there are plenty of people who have nine-to-five jobs and receive a fixed annual salary, which isn't going to change whether they're completing the tasks at hand or surfing the Internet. With salespeople, it's completely different. For me, when I'm not selling, I'm not making money, which means I'm actually losing money I could have been bringing in. In light of this, the most important word in my vocabulary is *efficiency*. I consider it a lifestyle that applies to both my professional and personal lives. As everyone in my family will tell you, I repeat this word over and over. I may use it when I'm teaching my daughters to make the best use of their time when selling homes or when we're all getting ready to go to the airport for a vacation. If you're standing in front of the mirror for an extra twenty minutes debating which pair of jeans to wear, that's wasted time. If you lay out your clothing the night before—*that* is efficient.

THE ENTREPRENEUR BUG

Becoming a salesperson is one thing. Catching the entrepreneur bug is quite another. The two can exist independently or together, but the latter requires the determination to find new and lucrative opportunities. For me, they're absolutely cojoined. Yes, selling was an immediate passion. But expanding was an even greater passion and one that I couldn't deny.

A perfect example of this is the time I was at a textile show selling piece goods for my father's company, and one of our customers suggested I check out a fashion brand called 90265. He said they were a very small company and that they needed help. He then introduced me to the owners, who shared that they were only selling about $300,000 per year and that they needed to grow in order to make money and stay in business. As it happened, their clothing—which was women's activewear—was being made from the fabrics I was selling, which turned on a light bulb in my head. I figured that my father's company could probably acquire 90265 and finance it through our own fabrics by offering good terms for payment, because their main problem was cash flow.

So, I went back to my father and presented the opportunity, which he supported. Not only did he think it would be a great new source of income for us, but he also appreciated the fact that I was thinking like an entrepreneur. Under my direction, we created a larger sales force, which allowed us to increase our production and credit and subsequently buy more piece goods. We also broadened our sales from local stores to big retailers like JCPenney, The Limited, Nordstrom, Macy's, Bloomingdale's, and Saks Fifth Avenue. By expanding in this way, we took 90265 from $300,000 in sales to roughly $30 million in the first two years, which was pretty unbelievable.

Unfortunately, when you garment-dye clothing as we were doing, which was very cool and ahead of its time, you can't control how much it will shrink, and therefore a size medium could vary immensely from one sweatshirt to another. This might have been okay for the smaller boutiques, but for the bigger stores it was not. And they ended up returning many of the goods, which made it unsustainable for us.

The good news is that this lesson did not dampen my entrepreneurial spirit at all. We'd done the best we could do with 90265, and it was time to sell it to a company that could take it to the next level.

TRUST YOUR INSTINCT

Once we realized that 90265 was no longer going to be profitable for us, we sold it to another manufacturer that was doing a lot of private labels for big-box stores such as Target, and I left my father's company to go work for them, which he was very supportive of. Retailers like Target, Ross Dress for Less, and T.J.Maxx, to name a few, often need brands that are "faulty," so to speak, which doesn't mean there's anything really wrong with the product; it's typically just small idiosyncrasies that make it impossible for them to sell the garment at full price, with full disclosure that there are slight imperfections. Still, there has to be a label.

As it happens, after a brief period of working for them, I realized that I didn't love my bosses, it wasn't a fun job for me, and I definitely wasn't passionate about it.

I think a lot of people make the mistake of staying in positions that don't motivate them. By no means am I suggesting that anyone who doesn't like their job should up and quit. But I do think that, if you're unhappy, you have to trust your instinct and search for something that will fulfill you. What you do for work accounts for too many hours in the day for you to be miserable. And, if you're disgruntled, or even apathetic, it will impact all areas of your life. For me, that's an unbearable way to live. If something doesn't feel right, then it's usually not right and it's time to start looking for a new job that will inspire you every day and in the long term.

CLIMB THE LADDER

At this point in my career, I was focused on continuing to grow and to climb the corporate ladder as quickly as I could. I knew I had a lot to offer and, as always, the confidence my parents instilled in me from a very early age allowed me to have faith that I could accomplish anything I set my mind to. So I left 90265 and went to work for Carole Little, the largest fashion manufacturing company in Los Angeles, possibly in the entire country. At the time, they were struggling to stay current, and they offered me an amazing opportunity to start a division for them, which was in essence knocking off 90265, my former brand.

Prior to joining Carole Little, I'd never worked at a huge corporation, and I really didn't know how to maneuver myself through what felt like a lot of red tape and a stringent structure. Further, the tricky part of my new position was that they worked only with woven fabrics and my garments at 90265 were made of knit, which is completely different. I tried to tell them that it didn't make any sense to copy something but make it with another fabric, yet they were insistent, so I tried and failed, as I'd expected. It was a total disaster.

Since I'm anything but a quitter, I kept pushing for them to let me do my thing the proper way, which is what they had hired me for, but they weren't having it. To me, it seemed to

23

be an archaic method of operating that didn't allow them to compromise, even if it was for their own benefit. We simply didn't see eye to eye, and, in the end, they fired me after only seven months, right before Hanukkah and Christmas. Little did I know it was a blessing in disguise—although it certainly didn't feel that way.

MAURICIO'S MANTRAS

- When considering the importance of margins, every cent, as opposed to every dollar, counts.

- If you're a strong and motivated salesperson, you can sell anything.

- When you're not selling, you're losing money. Learning to be efficient is a lifestyle.

- Becoming a salesperson is one thing. Catching the entrepreneur bug is quite another. The latter requires the determination to find new and lucrative opportunities.

- If you're unhappy in your job, you have to trust your instinct and search for something that will fulfill you.

CHAPTER 2

FIND THE PERFECT PARTNER

Our soulmate is someone who shares our deepest
longings, our sense of direction. When we're two
balloons, and together our direction is up, chances
are we've found the right person. Our soulmate is
the one who makes life come to life.

—Richard Bach, bestselling author
of *Jonathan Livingston Seagull*

FOLLOW YOUR HEART

As the saying goes, "All work and no play makes Jack a dull
boy." I couldn't agree more. Even though I am very committed
to my career, I always make time to have fun. It goes back to the
concept of balance my grandfather instilled in me.

So, in 1994, while I was still running 90265 (before I went
to work for and eventually got fired from Carole Little), I met
my wife, Kyle, very unintentionally. I was twenty-four years old

and definitely not looking for a long-term relationship. A close friend of hers liked the clothing I was selling and would come to the warehouse pretty regularly to buy stuff. One day she said to me, "Hey, I'm going out tonight to celebrate a friend's birthday at Bar One, why don't you come with us?"

I didn't know that her friend was Kyle, nor did I really talk to Kyle at the party, but I certainly noticed her. After that, I saw her at the gym where we both worked out, and everybody would tell me that she was Demi Moore's sister (which she's not!). I thought she was gorgeous, and approaching her felt impossible.

As luck would have it, three months later, at the same nightclub, I finally met Kyle again. At the time, I didn't know that she was engaged to someone else, so we sat and talked for an hour and a half, and it was the most amazing conversation.

A few weeks later, I ran into Kyle a third time at Bar One and invited her to lunch the next day. A friend once told me that if you like a girl, you should always invite her to lunch, not dinner. Lunch means you want to see her during the day rather than at night, which is an important distinction, because it suggests that you're not looking to sleep with her. I'm not sure if that's actually true, but it worked out well for me either way!

At that lunch I fell in love with Kyle instantly. We had this undeniable connection, and the sparks were flying. I knew then and there that I couldn't let such a perfect woman get away, even though I was leaving immediately after for a weeklong vacation to Acapulco, where I thought about her constantly. When I came back, I called her. By that point, she'd broken off her engagement, and we saw each other literally every day. Very quickly, I knew that Kyle was everything I wanted in a woman and that we'd have a beautiful life together.

As Kyle and I continued to get to know each other, especially once I'd met her daughter Farrah, I got a glimpse of what a fantastic mother she was, which, if you think about it, is a real gift when you're dating someone, because it eliminates that curiosity and uncertainty of how maternal that person will be when you have kids together. It also forced me to take our bond very seriously, which wasn't necessarily my plan. I'd just gotten out of a lengthy relationship and had no intention of jumping into another one that soon. But I also knew I couldn't string Kyle along for two or three years while her daughter got older and older and then break up with her. So it made everything very real for me in the best way possible.

Another crucial aspect of my courtship with Kyle was her willingness to convert to Judaism so we could raise our future children under one faith. That was extremely important to me, and she totally embraced it. I remember her saying that all of her friends growing up were Jewish and that she'd always dreamed about being Jewish. Having that conversation early on was essential for me in order to take things to the next level and ultimately propose to Kyle.

WEDDED BLISS

I was twenty-four years old when Kyle and I got engaged at Shutters on the Beach in Santa Monica, which was definitely younger than I expected, but—as I said—I'd fallen head over heels in love with not only Kyle but with Farrah as well.

At this point in my life, my career certainly wasn't as prosperous as it is today and, therefore, neither was my financial security. Thankfully, my mother gave me some money she'd stashed away so I could buy Kyle a beautiful ring, which I hid in a box that looked like a rose, among two dozen real roses. At first, Kyle didn't realize that one of the roses was actually a box, until finally I said to her, "Did you notice this rose smells completely different than the others?" Then I got down on one knee and proposed. Kyle was so surprised and ecstatic—obviously she said yes!

On January 20, 1996, we were married at Bel-Air Country Club in Los Angeles, in front of roughly 250 family and friends, and our photos were taken at Barron Hilton's estate in Holmby Hills, which was spectacular. We had a Jewish ceremony and a super-fun reception where everyone danced and drank into the early-morning hours. It was one of the best days of our lives and filled with so much passion.

Unfortunately, years later, Kyle lost her engagement ring while taping an episode of *ER*. She put it in her pocket, because she couldn't wear it during filming, and when she took off her nurse costume, the ring went to the laundry with it. Of course we were very sad, since it was sentimental, but I'd started making a bit more money by then, so I was able to replace it. The truth is, as long as you have your health and your loved ones, superficial possessions are just that, and losing them shouldn't impact your life in a major way.

FATHERHOOD

What many people don't know is that our wedding was originally scheduled for May 1996, but we ended up moving it up four months to January because Kyle was pregnant!

Even before we got married, we'd talked a lot about wanting to have children right away, in part because we already had Farrah and wanted to give her a sibling relatively close in age. While we were having those conversations, we took a trip to Las Vegas and we were hanging out with Mark Hughes, who was the owner of Herbalife together with Rick and Kathy Hilton and Adnan Khashoggi—a Saudi businessman, who at that point was one of the richest men in the world. We were all playing baccarat. (Well, Mark and Adnan were playing baccarat, gambling millions of dollars, and we were watching!) As it happened, Adnan traveled with a very big entourage, one of whom was his psychic. And this psychic told Kyle that she was going to have a really hard time getting pregnant again, which made her pretty unhappy, so much so that when we went up to our hotel room, she decided to stop taking birth control.

Apparently, Adnan's psychic wasn't always accurate, because Kyle got pregnant with Alexia that night. I'll never forget when she told me a few weeks later. We were out to dinner for a date night, and she actually showed me the positive pregnancy test. I was in total shock! But also extremely excited.

Very quickly we made arrangements to move the wedding from May to January so Kyle could fit in her dress. Fortunately, Kyle loved being pregnant. Her health was great, and she was such a trouper, especially given that I was so young and not always as empathetic as I could have been. I couldn't understand why she didn't want to ski with me while pregnant with Alexia—it was definitely a learning curve, but my compassion improved with each child!

On June 18 of the same year, Alexia Simone Umansky was born (her middle name is reflective of mine, which is Simon). Becoming a father was the most amazing thing that had ever happened to me. I was scared and nervous, mainly from a financial perspective—I wanted to make sure I could care for my family in the way I wanted to. But from an emotional perspective, I was overjoyed, and also thrilled that Farrah had a little sister, which was a surprise. We didn't find out the sex of any of our kids except Portia.

The funny thing is that, until a few years ago, Alexia didn't realize that Kyle was pregnant with her at our wedding. One day I said to her, "You realize that the difference between our anniversary and your birth is only five months. . . . What do you think about that?" It took her a few minutes to process what I was hinting at and then, suddenly, it hit her and she was like, "Oh my God!"

Four years after we had Alexia, Sophia came into the world, and eight years after that, my baby, Portia, was born.

One thing I will say about being a father at different stages in my life is that I've been able to enjoy and appreciate my role as a parent a lot more with Portia, because I'm older and more mature. With my other three girls, I feel like I blinked and they were grown up and on their own. Since Portia is only fourteen, I'm savoring every minute of it. Not only do I have more time to focus on her, but she's always there for me as well. Whenever I'm stressed or I'm simply not functioning as well as I'd like to be, I'll just walk into Portia's room and hug her. Then she hugs me back, and it literally puts me at rest. She's like the Mauricio whisperer from a mindset perspective. She's my medicine.

THE GOING WILL GET TOUGH

But before Sophia or Portia were even a glimmer in our eyes, Kyle and I were married, living in a two-bedroom condo with eight-year-old Farrah and six-month-old Alexia. And that was when I got fired from Carole Little. I'd been bringing in about

$180,000 a year and was making ends meet, but I definitely didn't have a savings account or a financial cushion to fall back on. The first thing that occurred to me was that I wasn't going to be able to buy Hanukkah and Christmas gifts for my family (we celebrate both). I was devastated and wasn't sure how I was going to tell my wife that I no longer had a job. I remember driving around the city streets aimlessly, crying my eyes out, which was very uncharacteristic for me. I'm not someone who typically engages in self-pity. I'm used to pulling myself up by my bootstraps and moving forward with renewed energy and determination. The thing is, when you're the only person you have to take care of or worry about, it's not that difficult to keep going, but when there are other people who depend on you— namely children—it's a very different emotion. I was terrified that I was going to let them down.

Eventually, I did go home, and as soon as I walked in the door, Kyle took one look at me and knew what had happened. I didn't have to say anything. Fortunately—and this is something I'm extremely grateful for—she could not have been more calming and supportive. She said, "You're fucking amazing. This is not a problem. We're going to get through this together, we're going to suffer together if we have to, and we're going to make something new happen for you."

There wasn't a single moment where she made me feel shitty for losing my job or implied that I'd done something wrong. She never asked, *What about me?* Or *What about the kids?* Or *What about Christmas?* Kyle was incredible, and she's still that way, which is another reason why I'm so confident in myself and in our marriage; it's also why it's so important to choose a loyal partner. Ultimately, she took it one step further by suggesting a new career path for me that would change both our lives (more on that in the next chapter).

As I said, the firing from Carole Little was a blessing in disguise. If I hadn't been let go from that position and Kyle hadn't been so encouraging, I'd probably still be in the clothing business today . . . or playing golf! This proves that, even when the going gets tough and you think you've hit rock bottom, there's always a way to recover, as long as you have faith in yourself and as long as the people you surround yourself with have faith in you too.

DON'T TAKE NO FOR AN ANSWER

Even in the early days of my relationship with Kyle, I always had a can-do attitude, and that confidence, which I keep coming back to, imbued me with the sense that I belonged wherever I wanted to be. I never believed that no was an answer I had to subscribe to. My feeling was that if I wanted to make things happen, all I had to do was find a way. And this sentiment applied beyond my career.

To this day, Kyle loves to tell the story of the time, in our early twenties, when we went to a very popular nightclub in

Los Angeles and they weren't letting anyone in. We were stand-ing in the back of a long line, and she was ready to throw in the towel. I turned to her and said, "Wait right here."

She then watched me scale a wall to get into the club. Once inside, I was able to charm the bouncer into letting Kyle in. Kyle says, "There I was, in total shock that he'd just done that, and suddenly his head popped out of the front door with the bouncer, who pointed to me and yelled, 'You, in the red dress, come in.' It was vintage Mauricio—he's always been completely determined and fearless!"

I want to be clear that "not taking no for an answer" doesn't mean you have to scale a wall or act in an aggressive manner. What it does mean is that you have to survey the situation, read the room (the same way I do when I'm selling), and develop a strategy to get what you want. You also have to be fearless, as Kyle said. In my mind, I ask myself: What's the worst that can happen? If you don't try, you can't succeed, right? And if you do try and you fail, that's it. I knew, in that moment, that if I could just speak to the bouncer and plead my case, he'd hear me. It turns out I was correct.

MAURICIO'S MANTRAS

- Even when you're completely committed to your career, you should always make time to have fun.

- As long as you have your health and your loved ones, superficial possessions are just that, and losing them shouldn't impact your life in a major way.

- Even though parenthood will likely be the most amazing thing that's ever happened to you and, from an emotional perspective, you'll feel endless joy, it's okay to be scared and nervous about the uncertainty that lies ahead.

- When the going gets tough, and you think you've hit rock bottom, there's always a way to recover.

- If you don't try, you can't succeed.

CHAPTER 3

PURSUE YOUR PASSION

I would rather die of passion than of boredom.

—Émile Zola

TRY NEW THINGS

After I got fired from Carole Little, Kyle suggested we get our real estate licenses together, for a number of reasons. For one, we'd often talked about how my true strength was in sales and—on top of that—our brother-in-law Rick Hilton owned a real estate company, which meant I'd likely be able to get a job working for him. Additionally, I've always loved interior design and architecture. So it really made perfect sense. And the fact that Kyle was willing to do it with me, even though it was not an interest of hers, definitely motivated me.

She said, "We'll make it our date night. I know this is your calling. It's all happening for a reason. Don't look at the negative; this is an important move, and it's going to be a better situation for you, for your future, and for our family. Let's make the best of it."

Her overall positivity and belief in me gave me all the courage I needed to alter my career path.

So we signed up for a class at Santa Monica College, where I'd gone for undergrad. It was once a week, and, as Kyle had proposed, we made it our date night, which was fun. Thankfully, we both passed our tests and got our licenses, although Kyle never put hers to use, because she was only doing it as a show of support for me. I think it's really significant to note that, when your partner is going through a big life change, providing that kind of encouragement can make all the difference. As I said, if not for Kyle's backing and constant reassurance, I'm not sure where I'd be today or what I'd be doing.

This doesn't mean it was an easy time for us, especially because I didn't have a job. In order for us to be able to make ends meet, Kyle's mom, my grandfather, and my father helped us out financially. We were very lucky to have family members to rely on. I'm well aware that this isn't the case for many people.

Happily, as soon as I set foot in that classroom, real estate became an extraordinary and immediate passion. I knew instantly that it was what I was born to do. There was no question. I understood the courses. I understood the sales capacity. Right off the bat, I got every bit of it, and there was no struggle involved; it fit like a custom-made glove, which was a great feeling. I believe that when you find that perfect vocation, you know it in your gut. It's not something you have to convince yourself of or something you have to rationalize to yourself. You just know.

Of course, most of the time, when you do land on that thing, you have to make sacrifices in order to get there, and you have to continue to sacrifice until it starts to become lucrative. Believe me when I tell you that the money does not roll in immediately. It took a long time before I was bringing in what I needed to in order to provide for my family in the way I wanted to. And during that period—in addition to the financial assistance from our family—Kyle was doing things like clipping coupons from local newspapers so she could save money on groceries, and she certainly wasn't shopping at Beverly Hills Market & Deli. She would drive much farther away to a less expensive store, where she knew the prices were cheaper and because she didn't want to run into any acquaintances.

Kyle also decided it was a good time for her to go back to work as an actress, and not only because of the extra salary. It was something she wanted to do, and I was tremendously supportive of that. She said she didn't feel good about herself without something of her own to focus on. I remember saying something along these lines to her multiple times: "Listen, I don't care if you work or you don't work. I'm going to support our family one way or another. But, what I don't want is for you to have any regrets. I would never stop you from pursuing your passion. By all means, you should get back out there, go to auditions, and feel good about yourself. If you make it again, great. If you don't make it again, who gives a shit? The point is that I don't want you to be fifty years old one day and think I held you back from doing something you love. That's the kind of circumstance that leads to resentment, which is the worst thing for a marriage."

And, sure enough, after five years of being unemployed, Kyle started picking up acting gigs again, like her recurring role on *ER*, which wasn't easy after such a long hiatus, but she was determined, which is a trait we have in common and that I respect deeply in her. We also needed the money, so it was helpful from that perspective as well.

The fact remains that if you don't put your mind and energy into what you truly enjoy, it's not going to happen. Success may not materialize overnight, or even as quickly as you'd like, but if you identify what you're passionate about, work hard at it, and have a significant other and/or family members who have your back, you can do whatever you set your mind to.

ALL IN THE FAMILY

When I got my real estate license, we were very close with Kyle's sister Kathy Hilton and our brother-in-law Rick. He and his partner, Jeff Hyland (owners of Hilton & Hyland) were aware of what I was doing, and whenever we would see them at parties and events they'd let me know that as soon as I was ready to go, there would be a job waiting for me in their firm. At the time, they had about fifteen people working for them, so it was a pretty small operation.

While I was very happy to be gainfully employed again, I made a promise to myself that, with each passing year, I'd make more and more money. I believe that you always have to challenge yourself in that way. Whether it's a financial challenge or some other kind of personal goal you set for yourself, if you want to grow and achieve, you have to give yourself benchmarks to hit.

Overall, working for Hilton & Hyland was an excellent experience. Both Rick and Jeff afforded me a lot of opportunities, even though there were also some road bumps. For example, one of the first houses I sold was to Kyle's ex-husband and Farrah's father, Guraish Aldjufrie. I remember being so excited about it. As it happened, he was under the weather the day the deal was closing, so I went to his house to explain all the paperwork for the property and the sale of the home. Farrah was there too, and it was kind of funny that all three of us were on one bed together. It was an extraordinary moment for her, because it gave her such confidence to see that her two dads got along so well. It's still that way to this day, which fostered a very solid upbringing for Farrah.

It also imbued me with great faith about my own relationship with Guraish, who'd hired me with the intention of helping us during a time when we were struggling financially. Although Farrah was only a child, she understood that we didn't have a lot to spare. She used to ask me, "When are we going to buy a bigger house?" And I would explain it like this: "We need ten 'cushions' in order to buy a house, and right now we only have two." In actuality we had zero, but I didn't want her to know that!

Every month or so she would revisit the subject and say, "How many cushions do we have now?" And I'd answer, "Well, now we have three." It went on like that for many years, which is why it was deeply disappointing when I went to cash my commission check for the sale of Guraish's home and, as I recall, Rick informed me that Guraish was his client, so I had to split it with him fifty-fifty. This was on top of the 20 percent that went to the firm. So, even though Guraish was actually my connection, whom I'd brought in, since he was Kyle's ex-husband and Farrah's father, I remember that Rick still asked me to do that, which did not feel good. I didn't know it yet, but it was an indication of things to come.

By the same token, there was nothing I could do about it, and I didn't want to look a gift horse in the mouth, so to speak. There was a development called Brentwood Country Estates that Rick's father was in charge of, and Rick gave me the chance to sit at those open houses every Saturday and Sunday for years, which allowed me to meet a lot of wealthy, influential clients who were spending upward of $10 million (that was a fortune back then; today that's the equivalent of about $30 million). My payout was small, but it was all about building my business and expanding my name recognition. I was very grateful for that, even though sometimes it felt like there was more taking than giving going on. It's important to understand that, while working for family comes with a lot of benefits, it can also be a tricky situation when it comes to fighting for what you believe is fair.

The good news is that for the next ten years, I crushed it for Hilton & Hyland. Before I decided to go out on my own, I was responsible for approximately 20 percent of their revenue. In light of this, I knew I had some leverage to ask for what I really wanted, which was to become a partner in the firm. At the time, around late 2007, Rick was living in New York City and wasn't as involved with the day-to-day operations of the company. He had his hand in other ventures, so Jeff Hyland was running things. Still, since Rick was my brother-in-law, I went to him and said, "Hey, listen, I think I've been killing it for you guys, and we're family. I'd like to see if there's a way for me to become partners with you and Jeff. I want to help you grow the business."

Rick's daughter Paris Hilton was on top of the world, and I knew that their last name carried more weight than it ever had before. I explained to him that we could franchise the Hilton & Hyland brand and become a global sensation. I said I'd be the driving force and do it all. Not only was it an amazing prospect for everyone, but—little did anyone know, including me—it was also the future playbook for The Agency.

Rick really liked the idea, as did Jeff Hyland. As I recollect, he came back to me and said they were willing to make me a partner, but the most they could offer was a percentage of top-line revenue, not equity in the company. He said it would be too messy for me to have a stake in the firm because of accounting issues and access to their books—I'm not sure why, and it wasn't necessarily what I'd had in mind (nor is it my business to speculate), but once I analyzed the situation, I realized that my main goal was to feel acknowledged for my hard work and success, so I accepted their deal.

The lesson here is that you should never be ashamed or embarrassed to pursue what you want, as long as you can prove that you deserve it. Whether it's a raise, stock, a promotion, or simply more creative freedom, if you don't ask for it, you won't receive it. You can't always wait for your boss to recognize your value. Take the time to put together a list of your attributes and all the things you've achieved for the company and then present it to your superior in an intelligent and respectful manner. Don't demand. Don't beg. And don't put down your colleagues in the process. Focus on yourself and why you should obtain whatever it is that you want to feel happy and recognized in your job.

BE A CONTRARIAN

In 2007, the Great Recession hit, which was the most historic economic downturn in the United States since the Great Depression; it lasted from December 2007 through June 2009, and then gave way to a worldwide recession that same year. This piercing financial decline had a drastic impact on the housing market, and the loss in real estate values was staggering. Volume dropped, prices dropped, and people weren't able to spend in the way they had prior to this catastrophic event.

Immediately, I was forced to ask myself: *What can I do to make money right now? And how am I going to take advantage of this turmoil in my industry?* I knew I had to do something to keep my head above water.

So, as I've often done throughout my life, I called on the sage advice of my grandfather, who said to me, "Mauricio, this is the moment to be the contrarian. You don't need to be the smartest, you don't need to have everything figured out, you don't need to buy at the lowest point, and you don't need to sell at the highest point, just buy when people are selling and sell when people are buying."

I understood how wise his words were, but I also knew that I didn't have enough money or credit to go purchase apartments or condos or multifamily houses. I had saved some money. I certainly wasn't starving. But between all the kids' expenses (at this point Kyle and I had four daughters), along with the overall cost of living, I simply didn't have enough to invest in real estate beyond the home we resided in. So, again, I said to myself, *What can I do that nobody else is doing?* And suddenly an idea popped into my head. I was well aware that all of my competitors had pulled back and that they'd stopped spending on things like marketing and advertising. I thought about my grandfather's counsel to be the contrarian and, with that in mind, I called up the *Los Angeles Times* and cut a deal with them to buy a dozen pages of advertising every week, which was expensive but within my budget. There were twenty pages in the real estate section and twelve of those were Mauricio Umansky. You opened up the newspaper and it was me, me, me.

As a result, the perception became that I was the only one busy selling real estate during the recession. People were losing money, which in many cases meant they needed to sell their houses, and my phone was ringing off the hook. I gained a lot of market share, and that really propelled me. I had such unbelievable success (when no one else did) that when I submitted my numbers to the *Wall Street Journal* at the end of the year, it came back that I was the number one agent in California and the number seven agent in the country. I was like, *Holy shit!*

But, at the same time, I also realized that I had only six spots to rise in order to be number one in the country. And, as awesome as that sounds, it didn't excite me. Instead, it made me feel like it had been too easy to get where I was and that the competition wasn't as steep as I'd thought. Strangely, it made no sense to me at all, although it did motivate me to want to do something bigger and better. I figured, if I can accomplish that by taking out a bunch of advertisements in a newspaper and I have all of these systems that are teachable and repeatable, then I should begin to really grow in the way I know I can. But I didn't want to do it alone. I wanted to do it with Rick and Jeff.

MAKE IT HAPPEN

Throughout the recession, I continued to kill it for Hilton & Hyland. Each year I would place as their number one agent, and I helped recruit other agents, which meant I was bringing in a ton of revenue in addition to my own soaring sales. To put it simply, I accomplished my mission in a big way. Even on Black Monday of 2008, while most of my competitors were bemoaning their deficit of deals, I closed the largest transaction of my life to that point.

I'd received the mandate to sell a beautiful property in Beverly Park, and a gentleman by the name of Ron Tutor, who owned Tutor-Saliba (now Tutor Perini)—one of the largest corporations in the country to develop airports, subways, bridges, stadiums, railroads, ports and harbors, hospitals, libraries, and commercial buildings—was the buyer. We were in escrow for the home because it was under construction and there were a lot of issues because it wasn't finished. Given that Ron had this major construction company, he decided he wanted to complete the project himself.

The Friday before Black Monday, we knew we were going to be closing escrow on Monday, which meant that Ron's money was due. I really liked Ron and wanted to do him a solid, so I called him and said, "It seems kind of silly for you to leave thirty million dollars in escrow that you're not earning interest on. Why don't you keep it in your bank account over the weekend; you can wire it on Monday, and we'll close on Tuesday instead."

As I recall, Ron's quick and concise response to me was, "Mauricio, when you're as rich as I am, interest over a weekend doesn't matter."

I certainly wasn't going to argue with that, so I let him send the money.

With that taken care of, I had a great weekend knowing that I was about to close on this amazing property. When Monday morning arrived, I woke up early and turned on the television to witness one of the most debilitating market crashes our country has ever experienced. I was freaking out, because I had no idea whether Ron's deal was going to happen. It had all transpired so quickly, and with the morning's devastating news that the economy was falling apart—especially in light of the fact that Los Angeles was three hours behind New York—I was concerned that Ron might try to stop the deal from going forward. I'd never experienced anything that financially catastrophic.

Then at 9:02 a.m. my phone rang, and it was the title company delivering the "good" news that we'd closed escrow. I truly couldn't believe it, especially because I knew I had to tell Ron, and I had no idea what I was going to say. I was well aware that it was not going to be a happy day for him—though he handled it like a champ—and he still lives in that house to this day.

KNOW YOUR WORTH

Black Monday was September 29, 2008. A couple of months later, when the year came to a close and my bonus was due, to my memory, Rick Hilton called me up and said, "This deal we made, where you get a percentage of top-line revenue, isn't really fair. Because of the recession, we didn't make any money this year, and now we have to pay you and write this big bonus check." Given all the hard work I'd expended, it was an extremely frustrating thing to hear, but I did understand where he was coming from, so I told him I'd think about it.

Two days later, I responded by saying, "I absolutely get the predicament you're in, and I have a solution. Let's just transfer what you owe me into equity. Make me a full partner, and from here on out I'll be in it with you through the best of times and the worst of times." This was what I'd wanted from the beginning anyway.

I added, "When we make money, we'll all make money. When we lose money, we'll all lose money. Let's just concentrate on building the company and franchising it out."

Disappointingly, as I recall, his answer was definitively "No, we're not doing that."

So I went home to Kyle and told her what had happened. She agreed with me that it was very unjust. But, ultimately, it didn't matter what we thought. In my opinion, Rick wasn't going to change his mind, and he wasn't prepared to pay me what I'd earned. In that moment, I realized that the circumstances were not within my control, very much in the same way getting fired from Carole Little had been out of my control. The silver lining, in both of those cases, was that the decisions that were made for me drove me to do something extraordinary. Had I not been let go from Carole Little, I never would have gotten my real estate license. I feel that had Rick made me a full partner in Hilton & Hyland, paid me what I deserved to be making, and showed me an inkling of professional love, I would have stayed. I believe I needed him to fail me in order to summon the wherewithal to pursue my dream, which was launching The Agency.

MAURICIO'S MANTRAS

- When you find the perfect vocation for you, you'll feel it in your gut. It won't be something you have to convince yourself of or something you have to rationalize to yourself. You'll just know.

- Success may not materialize overnight, or even as quickly as you'd like it to, but if you identify what you're passionate about, work hard at it, and have a significant other and/or family members who have your back, you can do whatever you set your mind to.

- Whether it's a financial challenge or some other kind of personal goal you outline for yourself, if you want to grow and achieve, you have to give yourself benchmarks to hit.

- While working for family comes with a lot of benefits, it can also be a tricky situation when it comes to fighting for what you believe is fair.

- You can't always wait for your boss to recognize your value. Whether it's a raise, equity, a promotion, or simply more creative freedom, if you don't ask for it, you won't receive it.

- As my grandfather said, "You don't need to be the smartest; just buy when people are selling and sell when people are buying."

- When decisions are out of your control or when people fail you, rather than allowing it to discourage you, switch gears and drive yourself to pursue something new and extraordinary.

CHAPTER 4

BE AN INNOVATOR, NOT AN IMITATOR

Innovation is the ability to see change as an
opportunity—not a threat.

—Steve Jobs, American entrepreneur,
inventor, and business magnate

WITHOUT RISK, THERE'S NO REWARD

With the knowledge that I could no longer stay at Hilton &
Hyland if I wasn't going to be paid appropriately or made a full
partner, I started planning to go out on my own. I knew there
would be plenty of risk involved in starting my own company,
especially when I had to leave the family business in order to
do that.

The first and most important thing I did was to ensure that
I had Kyle's blessing. As always, she was 100 percent supportive

of my decision and said that even if it made waves with Rick, she believed that I was completely justified in my desire to pursue my own path.

Once I had Kyle's approval, I began to think about taking on a partner in my new venture. I didn't feel like I could do it myself. Not because I was incapable but because I was self-aware. I know my strengths and weaknesses and my limitations in terms of my ability to get things done. I needed someone to collaborate with, to bat around ideas with, and to help me figure the whole thing out. In order to zero in on the ideal person, I analyzed the real estate market and wrote down a list of all the colleagues I respected, specifically the ones who possessed completely diverse characteristics and aptitudes from my own—but still somebody I felt shared my moral compass. In other words, the yin to my yang.

The name that kept rising to the top of that list was Billy Rose, and, for that reason, he was the first call I made. Billy had a number of attributes that complemented my skill set. He'd recently created a real estate networking group with the goal of sharing off-market listings and clients, which I was part of. We met once a week at a different house that one of us had a listing on, and we'd show the property, collaborate, and discuss the industry landscape. Billy was also an attorney and a real estate developer. And, at the time, he was the number one agent in LA for Berkshire Hathaway. Unlike me, he was outstanding with operations. He's the guy who dots every *i*, crosses every *t*, and keeps things moving forward. I'm more of a big thinker, an innovator, and a dreamer.

So I called Billy and invited him over to a new house I'd just bought in Bel Air to broach the subject of becoming my partner, though I didn't tell him that on the phone. I said I wanted him to see the place and run some ideas by him, which he later admitted he thought was a little fishy. The house was being remodeled, and the framing was kind of nasty, but it did have a pool table and I had a bottle of wine!

As we played pool and drank a little, I explained my idea for starting a new real estate firm. I said, "I need a partner in crime, and I want it to be you."

Right away, on the spot, he replied, "I'm in."

I was like, "Really? You don't want to think about it and get back to me?"

He said, "No, let's do this. We just need to come up with a great name."

I told him I already had one and that it was kind of a deal-breaker for me. Having worked for Hilton & Hyland, I knew I didn't want to name the company after myself or whomever it was I was running it with, like Umansky & Rose. It was very important to me that the name sound generic. My belief is that it's actually all the real estate agents at a firm who really represent the brand, and when they're advertising their houses, they shouldn't feel like they're advertising for the owner. From personal experience, I knew that every time I was spending money promoting my properties, I was effectively doing publicity for Rick Hilton and Jeff Hyland.

Billy understood immediately and asked, "Okay, well what is it?"

I said, "The Agency."

He smiled and responded, "I fucking love it."

A little known fact is that, in the beginning, we actually had a third partner, a female Realtor named Jade Mills, who's also amazing and a total badass. She really wanted to be a part of what we were doing, but—at the end of the day—I think she got scared to leave Coldwell Banker, as she was one of their top agents worldwide. I'm guessing that, in hindsight, she regrets that decision, but I believe she wasn't willing to take the risk, which I definitely understand. Forgoing financial security to gamble on an uncertain opportunity isn't for everyone, and fear of change is a very real and common phenomenon.

Thankfully, Billy did not possess that same apprehension, and it became clear to me immediately that he was the perfect partner for me. Almost on a daily basis, I'd get out of the shower (which is where I do most of my big thinking) and call him up and say things like, "Here's where we're going to be five years from now."

And he'd reply, "I don't know how you're going to get us there in five years. But I'm ready for the journey. By the way, what are we doing today?"

That kind of counterbalance was critical for me. Quite honestly, during our planning stage and even as things started moving along, there were many times throughout the process that I would have stopped because of my ADD. I wouldn't have taken that next step, and my grand thinking would have gone somewhere else. Gratefully, Billy wasn't having that. He didn't give me a choice. Every time I so much as paused, he outlined what was directly in front of us and put his foot on the gas, which was exactly what I needed to keep me going.

We knew it wasn't going to be easy and that there would be roadblocks along the way, but we also knew that if we didn't take the leap we'd remain stagnant.

BELIEVE IN YOURSELF

From that moment on, Billy and I both had 100 percent certainty about our common mission. We hired my brother-in-law Kendall Benton (my sister Sharon's husband), who was a business consultant and whom we trusted implicitly, to create a five-year plan for us based on our hopes and assumptions for future growth. Although I'm getting ahead of myself here, I'm extremely proud to say that we've hit every one of our projected milestones and beyond. Quite bluntly—we fucking nailed it! Between the number of agents, the amount of revenue, and everything else that we'd wished for, we've been within single-digit percentage points. And, honestly, shit like that doesn't always happen, so it's been truly extraordinary to live through it.

Of course, as it was happening, we had no idea of the massive success to come. What we did know was that we had a long road ahead and a steep mountain to climb. There were a lot of decisions to be made, and there were many times, despite our robust confidence, that we asked ourselves: *Should we keep going? Is what we're doing good enough?*

One of the things that we really wanted to go after were new-development projects. At the time, LA was not well known for this in the way that New York and Miami were, where you get a listing for anywhere from sixty to one hundred to three hundred condos, which means—as an agent—you can solidify a number of deals all at once, rather than piecemeal. In light of this, we wanted to set up a division devoted to new-development deals. As we began to research and talk to people within the industry, we heard that the Ritz-Carlton Residences in Los Angeles was looking to change their sales team. Since it was a recession, they were not doing well, and they wanted to bring in fresh blood. Billy and I felt certain that we were the right men for the job, but we were also well aware that the competition would be robust, if we could even get our foot in the door, because The Agency wasn't an established entity yet.

Regardless, with the appropriate amount of persistence, we landed a meeting with Ritz-Carlton and—although I was still

with Hilton & Hyland and Billy was still at Berkshire Hathaway—we represented ourselves as The Agency. Our reasoning
was that we weren't pitching the present, we were pitching the
future. We definitely knew that there was a chance our respective firms could find out, but there was nothing we could do
about it, and, more than that, it was a calculated risk we were
willing to take in order to land the business.

The amusing thing is that we didn't have anywhere near
the legs to stand on that our opponents had. Most of them
were large corporations. And there we were, two guys with a
wing and a prayer. We put together a brief plan, walked into
the Ritz-Carlton offices, and I said, "We're starting this new
company. I'm the number one real estate agent in California.
Billy is number one at Berkshire Hathaway. We're creating a
new-development division, and we're going to crush it for you
guys."

When we left the meeting, we were pretty sure they weren't
going to hire us, but it was fun trying! It wasn't that we didn't
believe in ourselves; we did. But we were also realistic and
we knew that, whatever the outcome was, we'd find a way to
achieve what we wanted.

Remarkably, we must have done something right, because
we got a call back for a second meeting. It was the Friday afternoon before Labor Day weekend and we went down to Anschutz
Entertainment Group (better known as AEG), which owns the
Ritz-Carlton in addition to multiple world-class arenas, stadi-

ums, clubs, sports teams (like the Los Angeles Lakers and the Los Angeles Kings), and so much more. Billy and I entered this big boardroom and sat down with Tim Leiweke, the president and CEO of AEG, and Sean Dee who was the president of global branding for AEG Live. They had a stack of unbelievably thorough RFPs (requests for proposal) from our competitors, which appeared to be as thick as encyclopedias and about 130 pages each. Billy and I were like, *What the hell are we doing here?*

But, before we could even comment, they said, "Well, guys, these are your competitors' proposals, and this is your proposal . . ."

To give you a sense of the disparity, ours was about five pages long, and it practically feathered down to the conference table.

They continued, "We have no idea why, but we want to go with you. When do you open The Agency?" Billy and I looked at each other and exchanged the silent acknowledgment that this was our final go/no-go decision. Then we turned back to Tim and Sean and—only because Monday was Labor Day—replied, in unison, "Tuesday."

When we left the room, we gave each other a well-deserved high five, and said, "Here we go!" Then we went to WP24, Wolfgang Puck's restaurant, located in the Ritz-Carlton at that time, sat at the bar, and outlined what needed to be done before Tuesday so we could open our doors.

The first thing on our list was to resign from our respective firms, which I knew would be especially challenging for me, since I was leaving the family business. I wasn't sure exactly how Rick and Jeff would react, but I had a sense that it wasn't going to be the simplest news to break. With that said, the time had come for me to spread my wings, and—in order to do that—I had to believe in myself and in my conviction that it was the most important professional decision I would ever make.

IT'S OKAY TO WALK AWAY

As the expression goes, all good things must come to an end. In my case, while one door was closing, another was opening to something bigger and better—the opportunity to start my own firm and grow it globally, as I'd been dreaming about for a long time. The only unfortunate aspect of my departure was that I didn't want to upset Rick or Jeff, which I knew was a very real possibility, despite the fact that—as I saw it—they'd given me no choice.

Since it was a holiday weekend, Rick was in New York with his family, and I was unable to nail Jeff down to meet in person, which is what I would have preferred to do. I didn't have the luxury of waiting, as we'd committed to launching The Agency the following Tuesday, so instead, I had to tell them over the phone that I was leaving Hilton & Hyland to pursue my own venture. Oftentimes in business, things don't go as planned or work out as neatly as you'd like them to. You have to be able to roll with the punches and make the best out of the situation, whatever it is.

When I first relayed the news, Jeff was very upset and immediately asked what he could do to keep me at the company. While I was flattered that he recognized my value, it was too little too late. I felt that they'd reneged on my pay, and I was done. It was that simple. For their part, they didn't see it that way. They couldn't understand how I could just make the decision overnight and not give them a chance to convince me otherwise. I remember saying to Rick, "I don't know what you're talking about. This was hardly an overnight decision. This has been going on for a long time. You and I became partners, and then you went back on it when the going got tough." In my estimation, they had basically kicked me out, albeit indirectly. I wasn't sure what they'd expected me to do, but—either way— they didn't like the way it went down. Though I will say that after the initial surprise, Rick seemed like he was okay with it. I later learned that was not the case.

With that uncomfortable conversation behind me, I sent in my official letter of resignation and vowed to extract myself and move forward with the proper regard for Rick and Jeff and the many opportunities they had afforded me over the years. I truly appreciated everything they'd done for me, and there were absolutely no negative feelings on my end. Holding on to frustration and resentment can be toxic; it doesn't benefit anyone, namely you. Letting go is the best course of action.

In order to stay true to this, Billy and I didn't try to recruit any of the other agents from our respective firms. That kind of behavior is not only disrespectful to your former employer but also the type of thing that will ruin your reputation. There's no need to act unethically in order to achieve your own goal, especially when family is involved.

We figured that if there were agents who wanted to come with us, they'd reach out on their own. And that's precisely what happened. As soon as I told my Hilton & Hyland group—The Umansky Team—what was happening, they all said they were following me. That included my daughter Farrah; my father, Eduardo; and Michelle Schwartz and Alejandro Aldrete (who were longtime friends of mine from Mexico). They were The Agency's first four agents aside from me and Billy. They trusted my vision and just went for it. I was their mentor.

The same thing happened with Billy. His partner Blair Chang—who played a critical role for us—came along, as did the whole Rose and Chang team from Berkshire Hathaway. In fact, as Billy was cleaning out his desk, there was an agent named Jeff Kohl, one of my favorite guys, who said to Billy, "Why are you leaving and where are you going?" Billy told him that he was starting The Agency with me, and Jeff literally packed up his shit on the spot, without knowing any more than that. He was like, "I'm going with you." He didn't ask a single question about our business plan or anything else. He just left that day and then told Berkshire Hathaway after the fact, and he's still with us.

From the onset, one of the things that was most important to me and to Billy in considering our team for The Agency was that we wanted to hire people who represented ethics and integrity. When Billy and I created our business plan, we actually manifested the exact group of agents we wanted by name. Paul Lester and Aileen Comora were two of the first agents on that list. I remember we took them to lunch and were telling them about our story and what we wanted to do. At the time, they were working at a competing firm. Not only did they sell a lot of homes and have amazing clients, but their reputations were strong. They did things differently than we did—they weren't loud about their business, and they didn't advertise themselves—but we liked that. We wanted people who approached things in ways that were unique to ours. Thankfully, Paul and Aileen loved what we were doing. Without hesitation, they wrote checks to become partners and came on board. Through the years, they've been such significant members of our team and truly outstanding ambassadors, which has been essential to our growth. I don't think we could have done it without them.

Two other partners we recruited were Ed Fitz and Deedee Howard. Ed is not only an outstanding person but he's also an exceptional agent. He caters to a very sophisticated clientele and has consistently placed in the top 1 percent of Realtors nationally. Deedee is also such an important human being for me. Back then, she represented a group of agents that was a little bit more old-school, more conservative, which was great.

Again, we wanted people who had similar ideologies to ours but possessed a diverse methodology at the same time. It's like assembling an NFL team; every player can't be a quarterback. You need individuals with distinctive talents, and that was Deedee in a nutshell. She still works for us and is one of those people who, if she calls, I drop everything I'm doing and answer the phone; she's got my ear.

Over the years, there have been a number of agents who've grown with The Agency and have performed outstandingly. A few of those names are: James Harris and David Parnes (from *Million Dollar Listing Los Angeles*) and Jon Grauman, who's on our new Netflix show *Buying Beverly Hills* (more on this later).

Additionally, there have been agents who've come from Hilton & Hyland looking for a job because they were leaving anyway, but I've still discouraged them from joining The Agency, even if they're very successful, because my intention is to keep the family dynamic intact for Kyle, for my kids, for their cousins, for all of us. That's way more important to me than whatever sales they'd bring in. There are enough agents to recruit in this world that they don't need to be from Hilton & Hyland. Also, I think it's a great firm to work for. They're super high end and have an excellent retention rate.

So, again, from my perspective, there's never been any bad blood between The Agency and Hilton & Hyland or with Rick or Jeff (who, sadly, passed away in 2022). What I did not expect was that, after he'd given my resignation more thought,

Rick stopped speaking to me, which extended to Kyle and our whole family. And of course his wife, Kathy—Kyle's sister—did the same. I'm not really sure what triggered that, except that they were extremely upset. They cut all communication and no longer invited us to Thanksgiving dinners or other holidays. The only reason I can come up with, because they always hosted clients and friends, is that they didn't want me to poach anyone. I never would have stolen a client from Rick, though maybe he didn't believe my motives were pure. He and Kathy held tremendous anger toward us, which is not the way I choose to live my life.

Naturally, Kyle was very hurt by their reaction, and it was a difficult pill for her to swallow. But, again, as she's been throughout our entire relationship, Kyle was unconditionally supportive of me. She's not only my wife; she's my best friend. It was also an interesting time in Kyle's life. *The Real Housewives of Beverly Hills* was in season two and really taking off, which gave her something major to focus on outside of the family drama, and she was busy doing her own thing. Her fame was growing, and she didn't need to exist as Kathy Hilton's sister or Paris Hilton's aunt anymore. She'd spent years in their shadows, when we had nothing and they were the well-known Hilton family. Then, all of a sudden, I had my own company and she was one of the stars of this reality show that was sweeping the nation.

The bottom line is that change is often a gift, even if it's not a change you asked for, and even if it may not seem that way at first.

STAND OUT IN THE PACK

Once I'd officially parted ways with Hilton & Hyland, it was time to center my energy on getting The Agency off the ground. Billy and I literally had to create something out of nothing more than a handful of agents and an innovative concept.

We didn't even have a location! So, the same weekend I resigned, I picked up the phone and called my cousin who was vacating his tiny little office space on South Beverly Drive, which was on top of a barbershop and an Indian restaurant, so it smelled like curry. But beggars can't be choosers—we were desperate. Thankfully, it was a great area, and I was able to lease it immediately on a handshake with my cousin. We moved in Tuesday, with little more than some rental furniture, and just like that, we were up and running.

Our commitment was to design a company that was all about culture. We didn't want to follow the typical model, which was every man/woman for him-/herself and tended to be more isolating. Billy and I had both read a book called *Delivering Happiness* by Tony Hsieh, the former CEO of Zappos; the premise was that by focusing on the happiness of your employees and helping them develop professionally and personally, you'll create a more successful corporate culture and you'll be happier too. Every time we interviewed a new agent, we gave them a copy and asked them to read it. We said, "If you don't believe in this, our firm is not the place for you." The ethos of The Agency was all about collaboration, delivering amazing service and experiences to your customers, and supporting each other in our pursuits. If someone wasn't completely on board with that, we knew they weren't going to be the right fit.

In the book, Tony Hsieh also talks about the importance of bosses being in the middle of the action and not tucked away in a corner. So Billy and I followed that suggestion as well by setting ourselves up in smaller front offices and leaving the larger back offices for our agents. We wanted to be in the heart of the whole operation and didn't even have ceilings or glass on our offices—the purpose was for everyone to hear everything we were saying; we had nothing to hide. We actually called the area Central Park; there was a bar and a Ping-Pong table, very much like a tech company, and the entire staff would gather there. Most traditional real estate firms have offices with closed doors, and the mentality is that agents don't want their colleagues to see their notes or listen to their conversations. Their feeling is, *These are my clients, and I own this shit.* Conversely, our style was cooperative. If one of us had a client who was looking for, let's say a four-million-dollar house in the flats of Beverly Hills, we shared it with everyone, because another one of us may have had a client who was selling their four million-dollar home. And when that happens, then you're representing both sides of the transaction, which is ideal. If someone made a sale, we celebrated. There was no jealousy or bitterness involved.

Billy and I were intent on fostering an environment where people enjoyed working together, where they appreciated collaboration, and—even though it was a job—we wanted there to be an element of fun as well. Back then, real estate was always sold like this: *The home has four bedrooms, three baths, marble countertops, Sub-Zero appliances, and a lovely backyard with a pool.* Thanks to a man named Mike Leipart—who came to work for The Agency after being senior vice president, national marketing director at ST Residential and is now our managing partner, new development—we were able to reimagine the conventional approach to real estate and extend that innovation beyond our office culture to the way we promoted our brand. Mike had a great mind for marketing, and he came up with the fresh approach to position properties as lifestyle stories. He encouraged us not to simply tick off the attributes of a home but to talk about the community surrounding the house, things like the coffee shop nearby, and to show videos of homeowners throwing parties or hosting barbecues. The objective was for our clients to feel the essence of what it would be like to live there, which nobody else was doing at that time.

The third thing we dedicated ourselves to, in addition to culture and marketing, was technology. We crafted a system for customer relationship management (CRM), which organized all of The Agency's interactions with both current and potential clients. There were other real estate companies making strides in technology around the same period, but we were the only ones to prioritize culture, marketing, and tech all at once—and that really set us apart from the pack.

ROLL UP YOUR SLEEVES

The one thing I will tell you is that—despite the fact that we were doing most everything correctly—starting a business from the ground up is not even remotely glamorous. It's an immense amount of hard work. Blood, sweat, tears, and then more of the same. Billy and I were working eighteen hours a day and sleeping six hours, if we were lucky. I'd be talking to him on the way home, after we'd just left the office, then I'd sit in the driveway of my house and say, "Okay, I'm going inside to have dinner. I'll call you back in an hour." I'd catch up with my family, eat with them, and then Billy and I would be back to work from 9 p.m. to 12:30 a.m. We couldn't stop innovating and coming up with new and exciting ideas. When you're truly invested in something, you want to give it everything you've got; you have to if you want it to be successful. That includes rolling up your sleeves and executing tasks you wouldn't typically engage in. As I said in the introduction to this book, Billy was making runs to the Home Depot so he could swap out toilet seats, and I was acting as the office valet, moving cars so our agents could get to their listings on time. I literally became Deedee Howard's personal valet!

Just because you're the boss and the one who's invested the money—one million dollars in our case—you can't avoid getting your hands dirty. It's actually quite the opposite. It was our responsibility to keep our staff happy, and anything short of that was unacceptable.

MAURICIO'S MANTRAS

- Forgoing financial security to gamble on an uncertain opportunity isn't for everyone, and fear of change is a very real and common phenomenon, but if you don't take a leap, you'll remain stagnant.

- Change is often a gift, even if it's not a change you asked for, and even if it may not seem that way at first.

- When the time comes to spread your wings, you have to believe in yourself and in your conviction that it will be the most important professional decision for you.

- Oftentimes in business, things don't go as planned or work out as neatly as you'd like them to. You have to be able to roll with the punches and make the best out of the situation, whatever it is.

- Holding on to frustration and resentment can be toxic; it doesn't benefit anyone, namely you. Letting go is the best course of action.

- There's no need to tear someone else down in order to achieve your own goal, especially when family is involved.

- Starting a business from the ground up is not even remotely glamorous. It's an immense amount of hard work. Blood, sweat, tears, and then more of the same.

- When you're truly invested in something, you have to give it everything you've got if you want it to be successful.

- Just because you're the boss and the one who's invested the money, you can't avoid rolling up your sleeves and getting your hands dirty.

CHAPTER 5

THE CUSTOMER IS (ALMOST) ALWAYS RIGHT

Customer service shouldn't just be a department, it
should be the entire company.

—Tony Hsieh, American Internet entrepreneur,
author, and venture capitalist

HONESTY IS THE BEST POLICY

There's a tendency for people in the sales and service industries to be somewhat dishonest with their customers, mainly
because they're afraid that the truth will upset them or that
they'll lose clients as a result. This is a big mistake. Let me give
you an example. A few days ago, I had a driver picking me up
from the airport. He was running late, so he called me and
said, "I'm five minutes away. I'll be right there." Ten minutes
passed, then twelve minutes, and he was nowhere in sight.

When I called him back to ask where he was, he answered: "I'm literally a minute away." After that, another six minutes went by. Clearly, he was worried that by admitting how far away he was I'd either be angry or I'd find another ride. Instead of just apologizing and being candid about his tardiness, he lied.

The problem with this is that, if I'd known he was about twenty minutes out, I could have done any number of things: gone to the restroom, gotten something to eat, returned some emails, or attended to other work commitments, but instead, I stood there on the sidewalk wasting my own time—and that made me more frustrated than the fact that he was behind schedule. So, essentially, his fear of being forthright backfired, and the outcome was exactly what he'd been trying to avoid in the first place.

In the real estate industry, this kind of circumstance occurs too frequently, especially when you're working with clients to sell their properties. Every homeowner thinks his house is the best house in the world. In fact, I've never talked to a single owner who thinks his house sucks. They simply don't exist. To take it one step further, most owners will tell you that their home is better than the one next door for any variety of reasons, and therefore, they believe their house will sell for more and should be priced higher.

Trust me when I tell you that you will never lose a listing because you're being honest. If the sellers think their house is worth $10 million, and it's really worth eight, be direct with them. Maybe say, "Listen, the market value of your home is eight million. If you want to try to sell it for ten, I'm happy to do that. I'm going to make my best effort, and I hope I'm wrong. I hope we do get ten. But I still have to give you my expert opinion in order to set expectations."

The reality is that if the house sells for two million dollars more, the agent's commission goes up and everyone wins. But, that's not a reason to mislead your client. Here's what happens if you go that route. You tell the homeowners that you agree with them that their house is worth $10 million, even though you know it's worth significantly less, because you don't want to upset them. Then, inevitably, the house receives no offers since it's overpriced. At this point, you've spent a bunch of money on marketing and advertising and can't change your tune or tell them that you informed them this would be the case, so you look like you didn't know your stuff and you lose the listing and the commission. It's called overpromising and underdelivering and it will come back to bite you every single time.

Additionally, because owners care so much about their homes, they always want feedback right away. And, in turn, real estate agents want to please their clients. So what they end up doing is lying to them. Perhaps they showed the house and everyone had an issue with the floor plan or said the kitchen needed to be updated. But instead of just being upfront about the responses, the agent will cover his or her ass and say the showing went really well. After years of witnessing agents employ this "strategy," I promise you—it's not effective, and it won't end well for either party involved.

Just recently, I was privy to the details of a lawsuit in which the plaintiff gave his deposition and contradicted himself repeatedly. Since he was dishonest about most everything, he couldn't keep his story straight. When he realized his mistakes, he desperately tried to backpedal, but it was too late. Conversely, the defendant in the case told the whole truth, even when something didn't necessarily look good for him. And, ultimately, he prevailed, because his testimony was believable.

This is exactly why honesty is the best policy. As Mark Twain said, "If you tell the truth, you don't have to remember anything." But, if for some reason, you do find yourself in a situation where you know you're going to disappoint a client and the onus is on you, always make the call before your client does, own your oversight, and ask how you can make it right.

CREATE AN EMOTIONAL MOMENT

In order to be a successful salesperson, you have to build strong relationships with your clients. And in order to build strong relationships with your clients, you have to pay attention to who those clients are and what their goals are. Take the time to ask them about their loved ones, their pets, and any special occasions in their lives. Maybe even recall a specific memory that will make them happy. But, first and foremost, as simple as it may sound, it's essential to remember your clients' names.

In my case, I built my entire practice off open houses. Some agents cold-call door-to-door, others "farm" a neighborhood, which means sending postcards to every mailbox in a specific area, and others rely on their sphere of influence if they're very well connected. They may have been the quarterback in high school or the homecoming king or queen, and their family has a wide network, which is great for them.

For me, that wasn't the scenario. So, as I said, my approach to building my career and my client roster was to go to open houses as often as possible, which was how I learned about available inventory. And, at those open houses, I would play a game, which was to glean as much information about the people looking at the homes as I could and then commit that information to memory—which started with their names. What prompted me to do this was that, whenever I went to other Realtors' open houses, I was shocked by how poor the service was. I'd walk in and, surprisingly, the agent would be sitting there reading a book or, if it was a Sunday, they'd be watching an NFL game or a golf match on TV. Sometimes they were dressed inappropriately or, even worse, didn't smell good. It was extraordinary to me. They'd barely look up before saying, "Hey, the sign-in sheets are over there. Let me know if you have any questions." Then I'd go through the house myself without any input or effort on the agent's behalf.

That was when I vowed to myself to adopt a completely different approach. When I was hosting an open house, I would arrive early and make sure I had a big sign. In the beginning of my career, open house signs were written by hand on a chalkboard, which looked like crap, because agents would erase the information on a previous house and rewrite the new information, which appeared messy and unclear. I was the first one in Los Angeles to change that up and print signs with large letters, so the address was crisp and clean, and there was an attractive-looking welcome note. I was always well dressed and full of energy. Often, twenty to thirty people would stop in, and my objective was to make an emotional connection with every client within the first thirty seconds of saying hello.

I'd start with, "Welcome, I'm Mauricio Umansky. What's your name? . . . John Smith. Great. And your kids? . . . Fred, Jack, and Amy, excellent; it's so nice to meet all of you. What are you looking for?" Three questions, boom, done. After that, I'd let them go and see the house.

Then the next person would come in and I'd ask them the same three questions too. And so on and so on. Eventually, I'd see John Smith and his family walking across the foyer into the next room and I'd say, "John, how'd you like that kitchen? Isn't it fabulous? Please let me know if there's anything I can do for you. Fred, Jack, and Amy, are you guys having fun? Do you

want to check out the backyard? You can play on the swing set."
And off they'd go.

I wasn't trying to close the deal at that point. I was just making that human connection. Then when the kids came back inside, I'd ask them if they enjoyed the swings and I'd ask their parents if they liked the house. If for some reason they weren't digging it, I'd inquire what it was about the home that didn't meet their needs or wants. As in, were they looking to be in a better school system? Were they hoping to find something smaller or larger? Did they want a pool or a tennis court? More often than not, if I could understand what they didn't like about the property, I could find another property that would suit them better. It was all about creating that personal moment and getting the client to open up.

I always tell people that real estate is just like matchmaking. The more inventory you know and the more you KYC (know your client) the faster you'll discover the perfect match. You might be able to do it in one shot or it might take thirty homes to nail the ideal fit, but once the client is impressed with your knowledge, they'll trust you to help them find their new home. Whether it's your own listing, an off-market listing, or a listing that's just on the MLS (multiple listing service), it's your job to bring it to their attention.

This approach can be applied to almost any industry, even beyond the sales arena. Whether you're in hospitality, banking, law, or medicine, knowledge is power. The more you know about your client, your consumer, or even your patient, the better equipped you'll be to meet their needs. These days it's not hard to find people online and to do your research about them. Through Facebook and Instagram alone, you can find out a lot about someone's likes and dislikes, which will give you a more profound understanding of the experience you want to deliver to them.

For example, when I'm staying at a fine hotel, if the staff has taken the time to discover that my favorite drink is tequila and they have a bottle waiting in my room for me, they've just impressed me right out of the gate. The same thing goes for private bankers. The more they understand about their clients, the easier it will be to advise them about maintaining the appropriate level of liquidity while investing in specific stocks and mutual funds.

Of course, you may not land the client the first time you meet them, so you have to make sure you're prepared the next time you see them. I keep most information about clients in my head, but I'll also jot down little notes on their sign-in sheet after they leave. *John Smith lives on Alta. He has three kids—Fred, Jack, and Amy. His wife's name is Sarah. Wants a six-bedroom home with a gourmet kitchen.*

This way, when John comes to another open house I'm at, I'll greet him and everyone in his family by name and reference some of his preferences, which always impresses clients. They're like, *Wow, this guy still remembers me; he must be on the ball.*

One of the biggest mistakes agents, and salespeople in general, commit is to not pay attention. When you're trying to sell a home, or anything for that matter, you have to treat it like a professional sport. For example, if you were getting ready to play in a football game, you'd lace up your cleats, put on your uniform and your helmet, and make sure your head was in the game. Well, that open house you're showing is the same. Get ready for it. Put on your dress shirt and tie. Know your stuff. And read the room. You can't do that unless you're aware of what's going on around you and the people you're interacting with.

The bottom line is that if you can create emotional connections with your clients, get them to share important details about themselves, and help them feel comfortable with you, that's when the magic happens.

STOP TALKING

A big part of paying attention is listening. And, in order to listen, you have to be able to shut your mouth. Believe it or not, this is easier said than done. Many salespeople have an innate instinct that entails showing off their expertise, and they think that delivering a lengthy monologue to their client is the most effective and efficient means of disseminating information and closing the deal. In my experience, this has not been the case.

I've found that the best way to display my knowledge is to, first, listen to what the customer has to say. Additionally, as they're speaking, you want to try to read between the lines and, when they're finished, insert a quick one-liner that indicates you've heard them and you get what they want. While talking endlessly might make *you* feel good, it probably won't make your client feel understood.

This lesson proved itself in a major way with Lady Gaga a few years ago. Kyle had filmed a music video with her and it just so happened that we were out in Las Vegas when she was doing a concert there, so Kyle reached out, and Lady Gaga invited us to attend. After the concert, she brought us backstage and started asking me about homes, which surprised me. She said she was a huge fan, loved *The Real Housewives of Beverly Hills,* and was super interested in real estate. She also mentioned that, since she was so young, she'd never purchased a truly important property of her own. She continued by explaining exactly what she was looking for. Instead of taking the opportunity to boast about my success or tell her about my current listings, I sat quietly and listened intently to everything she had to say. When she was finished, I replied, "I only know one house that fits your description." I pulled it up on my phone, without even asking her how much she was willing to spend, and she bought that home, which she still lives in today.

The point here is, if I'd been more focused on proving myself to her and touting my own accolades rather than figur-

Baby Mauricio with his parents.

A young Mauricio at a country club in Mexico City in 1974.

A young Mauricio on a golf course in Acapulco.

Mauricio and his father at Disneyland.

Mauricio at eight years old in Acapulco.

Mauricio receiving a baseball award.

Mauricio and his sister, Sharon, with their grandparents Abraham and Olga in 1980.

Mauricio and his family during his bar mitzvah trip to Europe in 1983.

A family vacation in Vail,
Colorado, in 1988.

Mauricio training for
competitive skiing in
Vail, Colorado.

Mauricio with his parents, Estella and Eduardo, and sister,
Sharon, on a family ski trip in Vail, Colorado.

Mauricio and Kyle in 1994.

Mauricio and Kyle at Mauricio's twenty-fifth birthday party.

Mauricio at twenty-six years old with Farrah and baby Alexia.

Mauricio wearing a 90265 tank top with Farrah and Kyle.

Mauricio with six-year-old Farrah.

Mauricio, Kyle, Farrah, and Alexia in their first
home, a two-bedroom condo.

Mauricio and Kyle
at a New Year's
Eve party in 2000.

Mauricio and his
grandmother Olga.

Mauricio, Kyle, and Portia
at Victory Ranch, Utah.

Mauricio at the White House for a National Hispanic Month event.

Mauricio and Portia.

Mauricio speaking at The Agency's seventh anniversary party, held at his home in Encino.

Mauricio speaking at the first The Agency Forum in 2019, a multiday conference bringing together agents from all of The Agency's offices.
COURTESY OF THE AGENCY

Mauricio and his mom, Estella, circa 2014.

Mauricio in Times Square as The Agency billboard lights up behind him. COURTESY OF THE AGENCY

Mauricio and his sister, Sharon, at The Agency Forum in 2021.

Family trip in New York.

Mauricio and Alexia at the top of Highland Bowl in Aspen, at the end of an annual hike on New Year's Day, a tradition for the father-daughter duo.

Mauricio bartending for a Habitat for Humanity fundraiser in Boston in 2021. COURTESY OF THE AGENCY

The cast of *Buying Beverly Hills* at the Netflix Open House event.
COURTESY OF NETFLIX

Mauricio at Over The Edge, The Agency fundraiser for Giveback Homes, in 2021.
COURTESY OF THE AGENCY

Alexia and Mauricio at a *Buying Beverly Hills* press event.

Mauricio as Hugh Hefner and Kyle as a Playboy Bunny at the 2018 Farrahween, Farrah's thirtieth birthday party.

Mauricio on stage at The Agency's 2021 Forum, with more than thirty offices represented. COURTESY OF THE AGENCY

The ladies appearing together at *Watch What Happens Live*.

Mauricio enjoying one of his favorite activities, walking Storm in Aspen.

Mauricio enjoying a meal with Sophia in Aspen.

Mauricio kicking off Forum 2022, with more than sixty-five offices in attendance.

COURTESY OF THE AGENCY

Of course, if you're going to correct a client or suggest that they might not have the full picture, you have to be sure of yourself and certain that you're right. About fifteen years ago, there was a circumstance when I was not well-informed, and I'll never live it down. The client, Andrew Frame—the founder and CEO of the Citizen app, the Internet's fastest-growing crime-fighting mobile app—was one of the original investors in a major technology conglomerate, and the first time I met him, he came to see a property on Nightingale Drive in the Bird Streets, which is a very exclusive area where many celebrities have taken up residence.

Andrew was extremely well-informed and well educated, which I didn't know initially, and he started questioning me about comps and other sales. He'd ask something like, "What did 9318 Robin Drive sell for?"

And I'd reply, "It sold for seven and a half million dollars."

Then he'd shake his head and say, "No, it didn't. It sold for seven and a quarter."

Or he'd ask, "How big is the home?"

And I'd answer, "Four thousand square feet." And he'd say, "Nope, it's three thousand eight hundred."

Andrew had all of these numbers committed to memory and was catching me on my mistakes. Immediately, both he and I realized that I wasn't on my game, which was uncharacteristic for me, and I was really pissed off at myself. I went home that day feeling like shit and was forced to remind myself that being informed is absolutely crucial, without exception. Even ing out what she desired, I probably would have walked away without a deal.

KNOW YOUR STUFF

While I do believe that paying attention and listening are key components to achieving success when selling anything, I also believe that you have to correct your clients if you feel they're misinformed. With that said, you have to do it in a respectful fashion so they don't think you're reprimanding them or telling them they're wrong. The most valuable way to go about this is to gather a tremendous amount of knowledge about your inventory. This includes specific details about each property you're representing—from the brand of the kitchen appliances to the shape and size of the swimming pool and everything in between. So, for example, if the client is comparing two homes and doesn't understand why one house is more expensive than the other, you can explain that while one kitchen is equipped with Viking appliances, the other has been engineered to perfection by the German manufacturer Bulthaup. Or maybe the client has a misconception about a home's floor plan and you can say to them, "I think you should look at the house, because it flows beautifully and has very high ceilings. If you see it in person you might feel differently. I happen to know the owner and can get you in for a showing whenever it works for you."

if you're an expert salesperson, you can't get cocky, because when you do, you forget to go back to the basics, and you start becoming unapprised.

This was one of those situations for me, and it woke me up.

Fortunately, I got lucky—which isn't always the case—and Andrew's agent called me up about another listing I had, which meant I got a second bite at the apple, and I was intent on proving my worth. There was no way I was going to let him think I didn't know my stuff or that I couldn't get the job done.

Incidentally, the home he was interested in was located in Bel Air and belonged to the singer Nick Lachey. So I went to meet with Andrew again, and I came thoroughly prepared. I was actually praying that he'd challenge me, because I knew everything. And, sure enough, he did. Only, this time, I was on it. He'd met his match! The result of this was twofold: (a) he bought the house (which had many offers on it, since it was so desirable), and (b) we ended up becoming friends. In fact, we're still friends to this day.

Not only did I get the deal done, but we did something very creative with the transaction, at Andrew's suggestion. Since he was one of the original investors in this major technology conglomerate, he offered to pay for part of the house with stock options—prior to the company's IPO. So Nick Lachey and I both received shares of this unbelievable corporation, which ended up exploding into an empire. At first Nick was a little skeptical, but he's thanking me now!

KEEP IN TOUCH

Relationships with clients are everything in the sales industry. Even if nothing's happening in the moment, you should still remain in close contact and check in from time to time. Maintaining that line of communication will ensure that your clients don't feel like your MO is: out of sight, out of mind.

This is especially relevant during recessionary markets. Often, if a house is overpriced, there will be very few showings and, therefore, zero action on it. When this happens, salespeople tend to fear calling their clients, because they're afraid to share bad news. But, in most cases, this makes things worse (and goes back to my point that honesty is the best policy).

I experienced this firsthand when I was selling textiles, before I launched my real estate career. Very frequently, an order would come in late and, when you're selling textiles, you're the one who needs to deliver that fabric to the manufacturer so they can sew, assemble, and print it, and then ultimately get it to the retailer. So this means that when the fabric order is running behind, the retailer isn't going to have it on schedule, which is particularly challenging in the fashion industry, because a season is only three months, and it's extremely detrimental to miss any part of that. In fact, most retailers will tell you it's the kiss of death, though it's not uncommon.

When I was younger and working for my dad, if I found out that an order was arriving two weeks late, I would avoid having the conversation with our manufacturer at all costs. And I discovered the hard way, by being screamed at on multiple occasions, that this was not the correct approach. My father would say, "Mauricio, you have to make the call and face the music whether you like it or not."

As with most things, he was right. What I also learned is that if I did notify our customers early, there were things they could do to make it better. Even though they were upset with me—and made that abundantly clear—they appreciated the brutal honesty, because it meant they could plan the assembly on a different schedule or tweak something that would help expedite the order. Being armed with as much information as possible was always a positive.

In the real estate industry, which—believe it or not is not as intense as the textile and fashion industries—salespeople generally try to avoid getting yelled at. So when there's no movement on a property, they just circumvent their client rather than picking up the phone and saying, "I'm really sorry to report that we're not getting any interest on your house. Here are the ads that came out. I've made seven calls on your behalf, but it's just a slow time." If you explain to your clients that you're working on it for them and check in every two weeks, they will appreciate you instead of blaming you. Because what you're doing is showing them that you're on it and that you're planning next steps to get the house sold. This demonstrates that you care.

On the flip side, if you dodge your clients, when you finally do connect with them, there's a good chance they're going to be irritated. Even if you have been doing your job, if they don't see or hear about it, they think nothing is progressing. That's the kind of behavior that gets you fired. When you stay in touch, your clients know you're paying attention and they feel like you're in it together. This gives them hope that you can save the deal, which means they'll likely let you extend their listing when it expires . . . and that's the goal.

DRESS ME SLOWLY, I'M IN A HURRY

I'm a big believer in the saying "Dress me slowly, I'm in a hurry" by Napoléon Bonaparte, which signifies that it's better to do something properly the first time, even if it's not done as quickly as you might like. And also that, when you rush or make hasty decisions, mistakes often occur, which will lead to more serious issues or a greater time investment in the long run.

For example, I've been wanting to grow The Agency from day one and, even though I feel like we've expanded extremely fast, the decisions that have gone into that evolution have been very tedious and slow.

One story I'm reminded of is centered around our "No Assholes" rule, where we had to take a big step backward in order to move forward. We had a top-producing agent who was crushing it for us, but even though this agent was bringing in a lot of money, he was a really bad fit for The Agency, culturally speaking. So Billy and I had to make the difficult decision, especially given the fact that our revenue was very tight, to let him go. He simply didn't possess the same integrity or moral compass that we prided ourselves on. We knew that firing him would mean we might not advance as quickly as we'd like, but we also knew that making the right decision would position us better in the long term. And, sure enough, we were correct. As soon as we parted ways with him, we got calls from a number of agents who said they'd been wanting to come work with us but didn't want to work with him. So, in the end, doing something that stunted our progress at the onset turned out to be much more profitable for us down the road.

Another situation where "Dress me slowly, I'm in a hurry" played an integral role was in our pursuit of the New York real estate market. If you look at the top agents in the country, they're always either in Manhattan or Beverly Hills, so the former is someplace we've always wanted The Agency to have a presence. About four or five years ago, we were presented with an extraordinary opportunity to take over a large brokerage that, in our opinion, was failing due to its poor management and realize immediate growth in Manhattan. We did our due diligence, and it was an amazing deal for us. We felt they were experiencing so much trouble internally that they were basically willing to give us the business and allow us to operate it if we paid them through revenue. It was a home run.

But, again, Billy and I looked at the culture of their company and the bandwidth that it would require for us to step in and, ultimately, we decided to pass. It simply didn't feel right, and we just weren't ready. In hindsight, it probably would have bankrupted us.

Furthermore, forgoing this opportunity led us to recently partner with another Manhattan company that shares our philosophies and is even stronger on the technology side (more on this later). The bottom line is that by taking our time and not rushing into that deal, we're now healthier for it, financially speaking.

MAURICIO'S MANTRAS

- Lead with honesty. Overpromising and underdelivering will come back to bite you every single time.

- In order to be a successful salesperson, you have to build strong relationships with your clients and get them to trust you, which requires paying attention to their needs and wants.

- It's more important to listen to your customers than it is to show off your own expertise. Sometimes, you have to be able to shut your mouth in order to achieve your goal.

- Being informed about your industry in general, your specific inventory or product, and also about comparable properties or merchandise is absolutely crucial.

- Don't lose relationships with your clients. Just because nothing's happening in the moment, you should still contact them to check in. It's imperative to always maintain an open line of communication.

- It's better to do something properly the first time, even if it's not done as quickly as you might like. When you rush or make hasty decisions, mistakes often occur, which will lead to more serious issues or a greater time investment in the long run.

CHAPTER 6

THE ART OF THE SELL

Don't measure yourself by what you have
accomplished, but by what you should have
accomplished with your ability.

—John Wooden,
American basketball player and coach

DARE TO DAYDREAM

One of the things I'm proud of is that I'm constantly evolving and learning new things about myself. And something I recently discovered is that I'm a daydreamer—a trait that allows me to analyze every single potential step in the many real estate deals I negotiate. The fact is, when you adopt an open-minded approach to a variety of circumstances, by examining all the feasible scenarios, you're prepared to respond to every conceivable outcome.

For me, it's all about putting myself in whatever situation I'm playing out in my head, whether it's a transaction to sell a home, an important phone call, or a challenging decision.

Daydreaming is a meditation of sorts, where you ask yourself, *If I do x—let's say, market a home with a specific campaign—what will the results be? Will I make money? Will I gain visibility? Will I reach my target audience?* You have to consider the positive and negative consequences and allow yourself to be both optimistic and pessimistic in order to truly set yourself up for success.

This tactic is also effective in competitive situations, like when I'm contending with other agents to represent a client. I think about every action that my opponent could take so that I'm always one step ahead and never caught off guard. It's very similar to playing chess. You have to exhaust all the possible developments before making your next move.

It's not always easy to find the time to daydream when you're busy, but if you can steal a few minutes here and there, while you're in the shower or going for a hike, it will ensure that you're prepared for whatever comes your way.

GO BIG OR GO HOME

As I mentioned earlier, at this stage in my career, I've sold the most homes in the country priced above $20 million and have also represented some of the world's most significant properties, including the Playboy Mansion, the first house in LA to sell over the $100 million mark, the Walt Disney estate, and residences owned by Michael Jackson, Michael Jordan, Prince, baseball star Barry Bonds, and George Santo Pietro (ex-husband of Linda Evans and Vanna White). This didn't happen overnight. It took me decades to build such an impressive client roster, and there are a handful of things that helped me do it.

First and foremost, in order to attract high-end and celebrity clients, you have to be in the game. In the real estate world, if you don't know who's looking, who's buying, who's selling, and where the powerful people live, you're not in the game, and therefore, you don't have a clue about what's really going on. When you do possess the necessary knowledge about the marketplace, you can call those powerful people directly and let them know you have a buyer for their home.

Let's take the Playboy Mansion for example, which was a property I received an RFP (request for proposal) for and then had to find a way to win the business. By this time, I was well respected enough as an agent that the client came to me, but the question is: How did I reach that point? The answers are: confidence, experience, and knowledge.

In the way of confidence, one of the things people really struggle with is "the ask," which is directly correlated to the fear of rejection. The thing you have to realize is that all of these influential people you're targeting are human beings just like the rest of us. One of the biggest problems is when people put celebrities on a pedestal and elevate them simply because they've achieved a certain degree of recognition in the public eye. Having been on *The Real Housewives of Beverly Hills* for so many years, I've dealt with this firsthand. I can tell when someone is regarding me as a regular person and, conversely, when someone is treating me like I'm untouchable. Without a doubt, I'm more attracted to and impressed by those who possess the confidence to approach me as their equal.

Where the experience and knowledge come in is the ability to sell a one-hundred-million-dollar house as opposed to a three-million-dollar house. There's a much smaller audience and pool of customers who can afford the former, so you have to possess the technique and the Rolodex to go out and find those buyers. This is a lot harder than casting a wide net in a sea full of fish. In order to sell big-ticket real estate—as I said earlier—you have to be a matchmaker. The more people you know, the greater chance you'll have of playing cupid. It also goes back to the concept of daydreaming. If you can access the part of your mind that will generate every possible outcome of a sale and who the best prospective buyers will be, then you really start to become an extraordinary salesperson.

On the other hand, if you don't have the ambition or the poise to think big and go after what you want, you might as well pack up and head home.

STAND UP FOR YOURSELF

In addition to thinking big, you have to learn to stand up for yourself. And, in order to do this, you often have to think outside the box, which means to deliberate in an unconventional manner and to consider things from a new or different perspective. A perfect example of when this happened for me was around 2009, just as the country was coming out of a major recession. It hadn't officially ended yet, but people were beginning to celebrate and show off their wealth again, which they hadn't been doing for a couple of years. In light of this, we decided to host a big event at a very impressive property we were listing, in order to attract buyers. One of the people we invited was a gentleman whose brother was a prominent businessman and later became a well-known political figure. By chance, said brother was moving to Los Angeles and searching for a home.

As it happened, when he came to see the house, he loved it and ended up making an offer. Then he hired, whom I deem to be, the most difficult inspector in the city, which I knew was going to present some challenges. For this reason, I made sure that I was present for every single thing involving the home. I listened to everything. I watched everything. And I didn't let anything slip through my fingers. It was a huge sale for me, especially since there'd just been a major recession, so I didn't allow anyone else, not even my assistant, to attend to anything.

I handled every piece of paperwork and didn't let the deal out of my sight for even a second.

When the inspector arrived, one of the first things he declared was that the house needed a replacement roof. I was completely confused. I said, "Forgive me, but why would the home need a new roof? The one it has is brand-new. It doesn't make any sense."

He replied, "Well, in order for this type of tile to be installed properly, each piece has to be dipped into water before it's put on the mortar and that wasn't done."

I questioned, "How would you know that wasn't done?"

And he responded smugly, "Because I'm an expert."

I couldn't believe what I was hearing. A new roof was going to cost upward of $500,000, which was undoubtedly going to ruin the deal. There was no way my seller was going for that. And I wasn't prepared to give in to this guy, namely because I wasn't convinced that what he was saying was accurate.

So I went up to the roof myself. As I was standing there on top of the house, I asked myself: *What the hell am I going to do to make this right?* Suddenly, I realized that the next-door neighbors were building a new house and that part of their process was to photograph their construction from the air. A light bulb turned on in my head, and I walked over to their construction office with a mission. Fortunately, I knew the builder and the general contractor and, as soon as I got there, they could tell I wasn't happy.

I said, "The inspector my buyer hired is absolutely crushing me and my deal. I don't know how I'm going to get through this thing. Listen, I know you guys have a helicopter and you're photographing your construction. Is there any way I can look through your photographs and see if what this guy is telling me is true?"

Thank God they agreed and let me do it.

Sure enough, as I scanned through the photos they'd taken, there was a picture of the roof in question being installed and the workmen with big tubs of water dunking the tiles. Even though I'd suspected I was correct, it was very gratifying to have the proof right there in my hands. I went from being super down and out to having a pep in my step.

I returned to the house I was selling, went over to the inspector, and said, "Let me ask you a question. You're telling me there's no way that this roof was installed properly, and you're willing to put your entire reputation on the line?"

He replied, "That's correct. It needs to be replaced."

I continued, "So, to be clear, you're saying it would be pretty much impossible for me to whip out a picture that will prove you're wrong?"

He nodded confidently. And, to his utter shock, I promptly presented him with the photo that ended up saving the deal.

What's crazy is that this guy was so frazzled by the fact that, as I saw it, I'd proved him wrong and he was forced to admit his mistake, I believe he ended up making another major error that was very costly for him. As he continued the inspection, he put a plug in every sink and bathtub, let the water run, and then turned it off to ensure there were no leaks. When he plugged the bar sink, he forgot about it and water started over-flowing and ultimately leaked through the ceiling and down to the lower level, which destroyed the ceiling itself and some other wood. He had to pay to have it fixed so there wouldn't be any mold, and that was not cheap!

Overall, I felt he was so pissed that his integrity had been questioned for good reason that he screwed himself even fur-ther. The irony is that, just recently, he said another house I was involved with needed a new roof. We fought back again and, to my mind, proved him wrong again. So he's still up to his shenanigans.

The lesson here is that most agents wouldn't have pos-sessed the shrewdness or the resourcefulness to approach these situations in the way I did. They would have accepted what the inspector said as fact. This goes to show that the more knowledgeable you are about every aspect of your career, the more you can challenge things when you don't feel like they're right. Experts in any given field, such as this inspector, are not always accurate in what they tell you. As long as you're experi-enced and well-informed, it's okay to stand up for yourself and your client.

DON'T BE A KNOW-IT-ALL

When I first started selling real estate, famed jewelry designer Glenn Spiro—who's not only one of the best salespeople I've ever known, but also one of my closest friends and most important mentors to this day—taught me the importance of not getting in the way of a deal. He explained that, too often, salespeople want to be heroes or show off by protecting their clients, but what they end up doing is screwing things up rather than facilitating the sale. Glenn really helped me understand how to be focused and driven and that great service and knowledgeability are two keys to success.

At the same time, while it's extremely important to be knowledgeable, that's very different from acting like you know it all, especially when you don't. In the same way that I've said honesty is the best policy, so is admitting when you're not informed about something. When you get caught up in concocting stories or, even worse, actual figures, people always find out, and then you look like a bigger jerk than if you'd just admitted you were ill-informed in the first place.

For instance, a while back I was connected to the American real estate developer Steve Wynn, well-known for his role in the luxury casino and hotel industry. He was selling a property in Bel Air that had already been represented by a few other agents who were unable to make a deal. When he got in touch with me, I suggested some changes to the listing that would make it more desirable, and I showed him some other homes he might be interested in buying.

I remember him talking about his own vast experience, how he built and ran all of his hotels, and the importance of specific things he was looking for. Steve has an uncanny aptitude for viewing properties and understanding them, right down to the specific details—everything from the layout, to the placement of a toilet, to the number of garbage cans in each room. What's truly unbelievable about this is that he's legally blind but can still describe everything about a space the minute he walks into it. He can see the beauty without actually seeing it.

In speaking with him during this time, I quickly realized that the knowledge he possessed was greater than my own, and that I had to be direct about my limitations. So when he asked me questions I didn't have definitive answers to, I replied very directly, "I have no idea." Rather than touting myself as the consummate expert, I accepted the fact that I was sitting with a client who had more experience than I did and realized that I could learn a number of things from him.

Many years later, when we were both vacationing in Europe at the same time, Steve invited me and my family on his spectacular yacht. He shared so many amazing stories with us, including one about our first interaction. He told my daughters that what drew him to me was my forthrightness about admitting that I didn't know everything and that this authenticity was the reason he hired me as his agent.

This goes to show that acknowledging your own vulnerability can be indispensable, because it's that vulnerability that makes you approachable.

EVERYBODY IS A VIP

The instinct to be both genuine and accessible is something that comes naturally to me. I've always been a people person—someone who shakes everyone's hands and looks everyone in the eyes. I also believe these are attributes that can be taught and learned, if you set your mind to them and really put yourself out there.

Too often, when people are engaged in conversation with someone, they're scanning the room for someone more important. I see this behavior all the time, specifically among salespeople, and even more specifically within the real estate trade. It may be a natural impulse, but it's still shitty. What's worse is when someone treats people in the service industry as if they're below them.

Trust me when I tell you that when you only focus your attention and efforts on those you feel can deliver you value or make you money, it will not go unnoticed. The old saying "Don't judge a book by its cover" is absolutely true. Just because someone isn't wearing fancy clothing or they're not driving an expensive car, doesn't mean they're insignificant. You never know who you're going to meet in any given circumstance and making incorrect assumptions based on outward appearance is a major mistake.

Today more than ever, there are extremely successful people who dress super casually—they don't necessarily opt for suits and ties anymore, like they did when they were first starting out. It used to be that, based on someone's outfit, you could discern whether they were a laborer or a professional, but that's no longer the case. In our current society, you could be talking to a billionaire who looks like he's homeless.

As a salesperson, it's critical to make everyone feel like a VIP. When you do this, the same level of respect will be granted in return, and it will help you in the long run. Of course, you can't do it for that reason, it's just the universe's way of maintaining balance. It's the same concept as being philanthropic. When you assume a social responsibility to give back to those less fortunate, that sends good karma in your direction. If you stop giving, you stop receiving.

Case in point, there was one sale in particular that I made because a valet parker introduced me to a buyer out of the goodness of his heart. And do you know what I did? I gave that valet parker a twelve-thousand-dollar referral fee. He wasn't expecting it, and he didn't make the introduction for that reason, but—because of his generosity—he benefited. Further, he would never have known I was a real estate agent if I hadn't talked to him and gotten to know him. That's just who I am, and it's been an enormous advantage to me throughout my career.

I find people interesting, and I treat everyone I encounter with the utmost respect, no matter who they are or how much money they have. I want to hear their stories and ask them questions. Just recently, Kyle and I went to a concert, and we purchased general admission tickets because the VIP section was sold out. Typically, I'd be in the VIP section, hanging out with celebrities, owners of multimillion-dollar corporations, and other business magnates. But instead of mingling with those people, I met a wide variety of thriving professionals— an anesthesiologist, a back doctor, a private-equity guy, and a yoga teacher. They were all equally as interesting to me as someone with a boldfaced name. And the possibility that one of them will eventually connect me with someone else who has an impact on my life is very feasible.

In fact, a few months ago I was in Amsterdam opening up the first international branch of The Agency (it was actually Glenn Spiro who shared with me the importance of developing an international brand). While I was there, I had a wonderful man who was driving me around. I started talking to him and inquiring about various things and, all of a sudden, he was telling me stories about how he works for all the five-star hotels in Amsterdam and drives around a number of celebrities and local billionaires. Immediately, I was like, *Holy shit, this might be my guy here,* which proves that you can never predict who "your guy" is going to be. As it turned out, he was the owner of the company, which I didn't know initially, because it didn't matter to me. I took his phone number and entered him into my database as a VIP, because he may very well be someone I call on in the future.

On the flip side, there was an instance a couple of years ago when Kyle and I were eating out at a restaurant and tennis legend Pete Sampras was dining at one of the tables next to us. I'm a big fan of his, so I wanted to go over and say hello, with no ulterior motive aside from making the connection. Kyle was a little embarrassed by my brazenness and also didn't want me to bother him, so she asked me not to approach him, and I listened. When we got home, I really regretted not meeting him in person.

I said to Kyle, "Honey, please don't try to change me. And please respect that I'm someone who likes to go up to people and make conversation, without any agenda. It's who I am, and owning that confidence is part of my character. I don't want to walk into a situation and second-guess whether or not I should be talking to somebody, even if that somebody is Pete Sampras."

The point is, getting to know people—no matter who they are or who you think they are—is the best way to expand your personal and professional networks. And you should never stifle that impulse.

STAY CALM AND CARRY ON

The ability to maintain your composure in any industry is a valuable asset, specifically when you're in sales and service. When you become frenzied, and your heart starts beating too fast, and you begin to get nervous for no reason, you react without thinking, which is never a good thing. Staying even-keeled will allow you to run through all of those daydreaming scenarios you've imagined, in addition to the many experiences you've already lived through, and make a quick decision that's in your best interest.

As I said, I've worked with plenty of A-list celebrities throughout my career, which has been fun, rewarding, lucrative . . . and sometimes complicated, depending on their personalities, but there was one specific experience that stands out as a special kind of challenge, because it forced me to protect my reputation and problem-solve in a way I never had before. It also reminded me of the value of remaining calm, which is something I learned while working in the textile industry.

Prior to representing a well-known 80s TV star, there were a few instances when I found myself on the opposite side of a deal from him. The first time, I was the buyer's agent for a house that he owned in Broad Beach, which is in Malibu. It was a $14 million transaction, and everything went very smoothly, which was a beautiful thing. The second time was when he purchased a home I was selling in Beverly Park, a gated community in Los Angeles known for its large homes and famous residents. Again, all went well.

As it happened, our paths kept intersecting and, eventually, we found ourselves across the table at a third transaction. I was representing the buyer on a house that he was selling in Malibu, and initially everything was fine. Until we went into escrow, and then things got really interesting—proof that little nuances do matter. There was a contract in place that outlined the furnishings this TV star planned to leave in the house—a desk, chairs, and a couple of other pieces, including, believe it or not, a massage table. Just as we were about to close escrow, he decided that he was going to take the furniture that he had promised to include in the deal.

So my buyer and I called his agent and said, "Listen, the contract is clear, and we're not moving forward unless we get the agreed-upon items and unless the house is properly repaired." (Which was another whole issue.) We suspected that he was bluffing because *who wouldn't close a $20 million transaction over a massage table?!* But, on our end, we weren't bluffing at all. My client really did want the house, he just didn't want to be jerked around. It was about the principle for him. Surprisingly, the TV star held firm so my client instructed me to send him a cancellation notice and ended up buying a more expensive house in Malibu. End of story. Or so I thought . . .

After the notice was sent, I went to go play golf. While I was on the eighth hole, I received a phone message from a number I didn't recognize and saw that the voice mail was quite lengthy, so I listened to it immediately and heard what I remember went something like this:

Mauricio, I think you are the lowest piece of shit on this earth. You're scum. You're vermin. What's lower than the earth? What is the lowest thing that I can think of? Nope, you're lower than that. You're a horrible human being. You're a piece of shit, and I'm going to make sure that everybody knows it.

This went on for about five minutes, as I stood there in shock. Once the TV star's rant was over, I knew that I couldn't have such a powerful person in Los Angeles think these terrible things about me, even though he was the one who, in my mind, didn't honor the contract. So at the turn onto the back nine, I called him back. His wife answered the phone, since he was so upset.

I said, "Hey, I just got your husband's message. I'd like to come over and talk to you and see how I can make things right. Clearly you guys have a misperception of me and how I work." Mind you, they were still living in the house I sold them in Beverly Park, so I knew exactly where they were.

She agreed, so I showered at the golf club to make sure I looked as presentable as possible and drove over there. When

I arrived, they greeted me and took me outside, where I let them vent. I didn't defend myself. I actually didn't say a word. I just sat there listening until they were tired of sharing their grievances. Then I explained my client's side of the story and indicated that it really wasn't my fault. I showed them the contract and the language about the furniture being part of the deal. I said, "All of these items were included in the agreed-upon price, and you guys didn't honor that. I gave all of your people warnings that we weren't playing around and you didn't pay attention. Also, the house was an absolute mess. I can tell you right now that if you were the buyer, and you walked into the house, you wouldn't have closed either. Put yourself in my client's shoes."

Fortunately, after about an hour and a half of conversations, that calmed them down. Then he said to me, "Well, by the way, you sold us this piece-of-shit house in Beverly Park. The air-conditioning doesn't work. There are all sorts of problems. We fucking hate it."

I replied calmly, "I have buyers in Beverly Park. If you don't like this house, I can get you out of it and probably make you some money."

They accepted.

So, I walked out of that meeting with the listing for their house in Beverly Park, and a few months later, I sold it to another client. In other words, I double-ended it and made more money than I would have on the Malibu property he was so angry with me about. They then became my clients and friends.

The lesson here is that people react in very different ways when someone confronts them. You have to learn not to take things personally but, instead, focus on what the best possible outcome will be for you. I'm in sales, and at the end of the day, I need to be able to sell a lot. The last thing I want is to destroy relationships, especially with someone as important as this TV star. My goal in going to their house to talk was to clear my reputation. That's the only thing I cared about at that particular moment. I think a lot of people would have been too fearful to even return his call. I knew that if I went to their home and heard what they had to say, I could fix it. Too many people automatically defend themselves and their actions, without hearing the other person out. The key to achieving success is to listen and show empathy. You don't always need to be right; you need to win the battle. From my perspective, I'm happy to be wrong. I'm not saying you should bend over backward on everything, but sometimes you need to read the room and act accordingly without the desire to be victorious. I knew the worst thing that could happen if I went to speak with him was that he'd tell me to fuck off, but I'd still leave with my character intact and a modicum of respect.

In the end, I walked away with much more than that, because I was armed with confidence and conviction.

WORK SMARTER, NOT HARDER

If there's one thing I'm sure of, it's that I work hard. But I don't stay busy for the sake of staying—or appearing—busy. Everything I do is efficient and has an immediate and desired result, which is why I can complete a hundred tasks in the time it takes for someone else to complete twenty.

There are people who will sit in front of their computer all day doing God knows what. They don't understand that just because they're putting in the hours doesn't mean they're being as productive as they could be. And productivity extends beyond the office environment.

Just as researching homes for sale is an efficient use of time, so is giving yourself time to go for a walk, or exercise, or spend time with your significant other and kids.

The other night, Kyle and I attended an event together, and we were connected the entire time. What we accomplished in those two hours went a long way in furthering our marital bond, because we were "working" smart versus being home together, sitting on the couch on our separate cell phones. Sure, we would have been together on the couch, but it wouldn't have been quality time. You have to nurture your relationship in the same way you nurture your career, so you don't end up pissing off your clients (or your partner) and therefore have to expend more energy to remedy the situation. That's when you start working harder.

The idea is not to pretend to give your loved ones attention, it's to *actually* give them attention, just as the idea isn't to sit behind a computer and pretend you're doing your job. If you don't have something constructive right in front of you, look for it. Go through the motions of what you could be doing to create business. In the sales world, that might be hand-writing sixty notes and dropping them off in people's mailboxes. Or knocking on the doors of prospective clients to introduce yourself. For me, efficiency is everything in life, whether you're closing a business deal, pursing a new venture, or packing for a vacation—you have to get it done quickly and capably.

THINK ON YOUR FEET

When I was growing up in my parents' home in Bel Air, my bedroom looked out across Stone Canyon, where there was this unbelievable house far off in the distance, on the opposite side of the canyon, that was literally framed by my window. I actually had to use binoculars to see it well. I didn't know this at the time, but the home belonged to basketball star Wilt Chamberlain. Fast-forward to early in my career, when I got a call saying that Wilt had passed away. His trustee asked me to come see the property so I could try to win the listing. As soon as I arrived, I knew it was the home I'd spent my entire childhood staring at, and when I was lucky enough to earn the opportunity to sell it, they left me in charge of the house. I had to do everything to get it in shape for the market—this meant cleaning and boxing up all of his stuff, including his amazing memorabilia collection, which he'd stored in his garage. It was a really fun project for me, especially at such a young age.

I'll never forget that the home had this famous sex dungeon, where he claimed he'd slept with twenty thousand women. (I believe that's now been proven mathematically impossible.) The room was shaped as an octagon with pink and purple velvet and mirrors all the way around. I later found out that they were two-way, so one side you could see through and the other side just looked like a regular mirror. Overall, the home had extraordinary architecture. It was built on a bunker, which was Wilt's vision, and everything was massive with super-high ceilings.

One day, I was there testing how things in the house worked so I could show it to prospective buyers, and he had this hot tub in the master bedroom at the foot of the bed. It was enormous, in order to fit him and probably multiple other people. The tub was equipped with a quick-fill button that would fill it with hot water set at precisely 103 degrees. You just hit the button and boom, the water would pour out of a huge pipe. So I turned it on to test it and, immediately, I realized it wouldn't turn off. I was watching it fill with water, ready to overflow. Even though I didn't plug the drain, it was draining slower than it was filling. And I was completely alone and going bananas. As I was staring out the window in a panic, I saw this big three-inch pipe leading into the roof, which I figured had to be the hot tub pipe. So I climbed onto the roof and followed the pipe all the way around the house until I found a valve that turned off the water—just in the nick of time.

Since I was able to think on my feet during a moment of intense pressure, no damage was done. I ended up selling the house to the creators of *The Simpsons*, who lived in it for many years, and it's now being sold again by a Realtor at The Agency. Remarkably, the home has been in my life since I was ten years old.

MAURICIO'S MANTRAS

- When you adopt an open-minded approach to a variety of circumstances, by examining all the feasible scenarios, you're prepared to respond to every conceivable outcome.

- In order to attract high-end and celebrity clients, you have to be in the game, which means you should know who's looking, who's buying, who's selling, and where the powerful people live.

- Experts in any given field are not always correct. The more knowledgeable you are about every aspect of your industry, the more you can challenge things when you don't feel like they're right.

- While it's extremely important to be knowledgeable, that's very different from acting like you know it all. In the same way that honesty is the best policy, so is admitting when you're not informed about something.

- Getting to know people—no matter who they are or who you think they are—is the best way to expand your personal and professional networks. You should never stifle this impulse.

- The ability to maintain your composure in any industry is a valuable asset, specifically when you're in sales and service.

- Don't stay busy for the sake of staying—or appearing—busy. Everything you do should be efficient and have an immediate and desired result.

- You have to be able to think on your feet during moments of intense pressure or else serious damage can be done.

CHAPTER 7

PROMOTE YOURSELF
AND YOUR BRAND

It takes twenty years to build a reputation and five
minutes to ruin it. If you think about that, you'll do
things differently.

—Warren Buffett,
chairman and CEO of Berkshire Hathaway

DRESS TO IMPRESS (WITH NO MESS)

How you present yourself is one of the most important aspects
of self-promotion. Again, you have to think of yourself as an
athlete suiting up for the big game and base your outfit on the
type of client you're meeting and the home you're showing. In
order to do this, you have to read the room—a concept I continue to revisit across multiple aspects of my professional and
personal lives. This includes getting to know your clients and

really understanding their vibe. If you can achieve this, it'll be much easier to figure out what to wear in any given circumstance.

One thing I always do is select my outfit according to the demographic of my client, even if that means overdressing on occasion. It's hard to go wrong with a nice suit and tie. That may be your version of a uniform. A football player wouldn't run onto the field in a dress to get his ass kicked by an offensive lineman; he'd put on his pads and his helmet—all the armor he needs.

From the perspective of a real estate agent, or any salesperson, you have to create the same focus when you're on the job, and that starts with your appearance. While we don't enforce a dress code at The Agency, we do encourage our agents to pay close attention to what they wear, which is something I do every single day. If, for example, I'm meeting an older, more conservative buyer, I'll stick with the suit and tie. If it's a young twentysomething tech guy, I'll probably opt for jeans and a T-shirt. And if it's a rock star, I will *not* dress like a rock star too; I'll select something unassuming, in black and gray tones or maybe a cool button-down, because—even when I choose to wear something casual—I always want to make sure that my clients view me as a trusted adviser.

When I hold open houses or have very special showings, I take it a step further and actually dress to the design of the property, because I want prospective buyers to feel like they're entering a very specific lifestyle. Let's say I'm representing a beach house in Malibu, then I'll go for white jeans and a flowy linen shirt. A while back, I had a listing for a ranch in Aspen, and I wore all Ralph Lauren. If I'm showing a house in Beverly Hills, with impeccable interior design, I may switch things up and wear colors that match the house. This way when people arrive at the home—and I look the part of someone who would live there—they can envision themselves in that atmosphere, because I'm embracing the environment and the community. If you stand out like a sore thumb, or even if you miscalculate whether to go formal or relaxed, it will be an immediate turn-off.

There was one time, I'm sorry to say, when I experienced this firsthand by losing a $150 million listing as a result of being underdressed, which the client shared with me after the fact. What's interesting about this particular circumstance is that I'd selected a gorgeous Brunello Cucinelli outfit—very high-end Italian pieces—that I thought was perfectly tailored to the situation. Unfortunately, a suit would have been a better decision, and it cost me the sale.

As a salesman, when it comes to fashion decisions, you really have to be a chameleon in how you portray yourself. Not only do you have to play the part by knowing your stuff, but you have to look the part in order to prove that you understand your clients' needs, wants, and overall ethos. You never want to leave anything to chance.

In addition to a thoughtful personal appearance, a flawless presentation of the home you're selling is absolutely vital. This includes how it smells too, which is why there's that cliché of having fresh cookies or something pleasantly aromatic baking in the oven when a property is being shown. Conversely, I've gone into houses that the seller has deemed "ready" and had to literally collect dirty laundry from the floor and clean up dog shit.

It's not always glamorous selling multimillion-dollar mansions!

EMBRACE TECHNOLOGY

In this day and age, you have to embrace technology as a means of self-promotion. The bigger your digital network and your social following are, the greater outreach you'll have, especially with younger generations. Just as you have to dress to a situation based on who your client is, you also have to understand how your buyers receive information. Is it by reading a newspaper or magazines and, if so, are they reading in print or online? Do they watch the news on television or on the Internet? Are they active on Facebook or Instagram or TikTok? It's essential to nail down the best and most efficient way of reaching your desired audience.

What we're seeing right now is that buyers in their twenties, and even early thirties, are communicating and gathering data through social media, specifically Instagram and TikTok, while slightly older consumers are more likely to use Facebook. Simply put, younger generations are all about multitasking. They can do homework, while watching a television show, surfing YouTube, laughing at a video on TikTok, and talking to thirty-six friends on Snapchat. And then still get straight As. It's unbelievable how much "kids" can do at once. My own daughters have definitely helped me understand how to entice these younger generations, to learn their language, and to operate at their speed with quick, smart, attention-grabbing videos that appeal to their sensibilities. They've taught me that you have to be consistent with your content, because sometimes it's the fifth, tenth, or even twentieth time someone sees something that reels them in.

We definitely get leads from social media and have made some very significant sales as a result of it, up to $25 million. Without a doubt, the majority of our business comes from our sphere of influence and our own client base, but if we can close a steadily increasing number of extra sales each year through a combination of Facebook, Instagram, and TikTok, that could become investible income. For example, if you make ten sales that total $250,000 one year and the next year, you make twelve sales, that's $300,000, which is a 20 percent increase. That $50,000 can be put back into the company and help you grow.

In the fast-paced world we live in, you have to constantly be innovating and evolving in the way you promote yourself.

At The Agency, we have a team devoted to digital marketing. Currently, they're in the process of developing technology to better capture the next generation. We're effectively creating artificial intelligence to help us find out more about the people who comment on our content. We believe that if we can assemble an understanding of who these individuals are and if they're looking to purchase real estate, we can connect with them through modern technology and expand that area of our business.

BUILD A NETWORK

If you don't target the right audience, there's no point in marketing or advertising. As I often say to new agents, you have to find your network and then figure out a way to make *your name* matter. Your paycheck is a direct reflection of your efforts.

When you're in sales, everyone is a potential buyer, and you want buyers to be able to reach you. This means your email address and phone number must be listed clearly on your website. For me, one of the pitfalls of being a real estate agent and on a successful TV show is that all of my information is public, so I receive a lot of pointless calls. But, by the same token, since I'm in the service industry, I need to be available to everybody.

Building a brand and a trusted name takes a long time, and it only takes a single mistake to destroy it, so you have to treat your reputation like gold. We're seeing it today with cancel culture where celebrities, politicians, and prominent businesspeople are committing one misstep or displaying one lapse in judgment and being completely ostracized because of it. The 80s TV star situation is a perfect example of this. I had to make things right with him because I didn't want that solitary circumstance to tarnish my good name.

As you grow your brand, it's best to pick a lane or two, really dig deep, and become an expert in those areas. In my industry, there are agents with extensive knowledge about various architectural periods and specific architects, such as Frank Lloyd Wright and Richard Neutra. Other agents may follow a different path and become respected advisers, with their proficiency being an exceptional level of knowledge.

Another essential component to amassing a network is the concept that each person you meet could lead to an opportunity—so it's really helpful to talk to people, listen with an open mind, and gather important details about them. It could be someone sitting next to you on an airplane, and it actually has been for me more than once. Just the other day, I got a call from a gentleman who'd been my seatmate on a trip I took a year and a half ago. He was calling to say they'd been ill-advised in a real estate transaction and wanted to hire me.

A few months back, on an airplane from Los Angeles to Aspen, I started talking to the young man next to me who seemed a little anxious. As we chatted, he began to relax, and he shared with me that he was a talent agent. Then I told him what I did and he said, "No way, my mother is a real estate agent in Birmingham, Michigan. Now I know who you are. I'm a fan. I'd love to make an introduction to my mom; she works for a great company."

I was like, "Excellent, I love it. Please put us in touch."

After that flight, he ended up making the introduction, I spoke with his mother, and she then introduced me to the owners of her company. Through that connection we ended up converting her company into a branch of The Agency, because they were the leaders in their industry and looking to make a change through a partnership. If not for my chance meeting on that airplane, we never would have collaborated with them, and they're currently one of our largest franchisees to date.

ACTIONS SPEAK LOUDER THAN WORDS

By creating extraordinary experiences for your clients, you're not only promoting the properties you're selling but you're effectively exposing your clients to the lifestyle they're seeking as well.

When we first started The Agency and took on the Ritz-Carlton Residences, in terms of value, the listings were priced 40 to 50 percent above everything else in downtown Los Angeles. At the time, the country was just coming out of the recession, and we were really struggling to attract buyers. One issue was that 35 to 40 percent of the residences were under contract and Ritz-Carlton wasn't releasing them, even though they were never going to close. Just because someone puts down a deposit doesn't always mean they're going to follow through with the purchase. So, we got approval from AEG to call everyone who was under contract and say, "Listen, we can either refund your deposit or you have to follow through with the acquisition." It was a very big decision to offer to pay back the deposits when that money was already in the bank, but we had to gain back the inventory in order to start fresh and make even more money.

Since AEG owns the Staples Center (now called Crypto.com Arena), along with the LA Lakers and the LA Kings, we knew that we had some major assets on our hands, which led us to the idea of using event marketing and brand collaborations as publicity tools to resell the residences.

We started arranging small gatherings of like-minded, networking individuals—for example, investment bankers from Morgan Stanley—and hosting luxury dinners in partnership with brands like the cognac Louis XIII and catered by Wolfgang Puck, who had a restaurant in the Ritz-Carlton Residences. The goal was to get these people to the property and also give them the opportunity to increase their own visibility.

There was one truly unique experience we hosted that really stands out in my mind, which included a very high net-worth group of about a dozen people. We set up a fabulous dinner and then took them through the tunnel that leads from the Ritz right onto the basketball court at the then Staples Center—the same tunnel that Kobe Bryant and the rest of the players used—to see the Lakers play. Since the Lakers were occupying their own locker room, we invited the twelve participants inside the Kings' locker room, where we had Lakers jerseys hanging in the lockers with each person's name on it. Then we walked up to the VIP suites and watched the game from there. Everyone was blown away.

When you offer something truly special that money can't necessarily buy, you grab people's attention in a big way and attract their business.

Another instance of a supercool event we held was our mega open house. We were attempting to sell this massive house with a huge motor court and an amazing garage and, therefore, trying to figuring out the best way to publicize it. So we called up Lamborghini and formed a marketing partnership with them where we were sharing clients. In other words, we were exposing their cars to our customers, and they were exposing our houses to their customers. We brought in fifteen different Lamborghinis and reached out to a bunch of car enthusiasts, so everyone could come see the gorgeous automobiles and the spectacular home, while experiencing the lifestyle for themselves. We ended up selling the house as a result of that event, so I guess our plan worked!

RULES ARE MEANT TO BE BROKEN

Throughout my career, I've discovered many fun and unique approaches to promoting both myself and The Agency. I've also been very clear about ways I did not want to promote myself or my business. But there are exceptions to almost every rule, and this story demonstrates that in spades.

A number of years ago, there was an agent named Marco Rufo, whom I really wanted to be part of The Agency, so I recruited him heavily. Marco was definitely interested in joining our team, so one evening I took him out to dinner and I said to him, "Listen, you're a brilliant guy, and I'd love nothing more than for you to come work with us. However, something I'm really struggling with is that we're a luxury brand and I know you like to promote yourself by putting your photograph on bus-bench ads." I explained, in the nicest way possible, that this wasn't really our thing, because we felt it was kind of tacky.

Marco took in my words and said to me, "Mauricio, let me tell you a story. I was a homeless man on the streets for years, doing drugs and wasting my life. I slept under the bridge in Santa Monica. I slept beneath freeways. And I slept on bus benches. One day, my best friend and I were on a drug run, and he was shot and killed. I almost got killed too. That was my turning point. It was the moment I told myself I had to change my life and get off the streets for good, which I did. When I ultimately became a Realtor, those bus-bench ads were not purely about promoting myself. I intentionally set them up in places where, as I'm driving home, I can see them. They're a constant reminder that I never want to sleep on those benches again."

I couldn't believe what Marco was telling me or how short-sighted I'd been. I said to him, "Marco, our rule about no bus-bench ads is officially changed. You should absolutely continue to promote yourself this way."

Today, Marco is the managing partner of our Pacific Palisades office and one of California's top real estate professionals. This goes to show that, not only should you give people the opportunity to do things that may seem foreign to you but also that certain rules are meant to be broken.

MAURICIO'S MANTRAS

- When you pay attention to your appearance and incorporate the environment and the community into the way your dress, clients will be able to envision themselves in that atmosphere.

- The bigger your digital network and your social media following are, the greater outreach you'll have, especially with younger generations.

- Building a brand and a trusted name takes a long time, and it only takes one mistake to destroy it, so you have to treat your reputation like gold.

- By creating extraordinary experiences for your clients, you're not only promoting the properties you're selling but you're effectively exposing your clients to the lifestyle they're seeking as well.

- Sometimes, you have to give people the opportunity to do things that may seem foreign to you, as there are exceptions to most every rule.

CHAPTER 8

MINDSET MATTERS

You see things, and you say "Why??" But I dream
things that never were, and I say "Why not?"
—George Bernard Shaw, Irish playwright and critic

MAKE EVERY DAY YOUR BEST

My philosophy is that when you love what you do, and it's something you're truly passionate about, you're always going to have the best day, which goes back to the confidence my parents and grandparents instilled in me as a child. It's all about your outlook, which is something that applies to every aspect of life. Some of my favorite hobbies are skiing, hiking, and playing golf, and one of the reasons I enjoy doing these things is that I'm truly happy in those moments. I have so many friends who get really pissed off and throw their clubs when they hit a bad shot or have an overall lousy day on the course, but not me.

Even if I'm not performing at top capacity, I'm still thinking to myself, *Wow, I'm so lucky to be out here right now. I could be stuck behind a desk in an office. Or not have the resources to partake in the activities that give me pleasure.* Rather than allowing myself to dwell on the negative, I choose to focus on the positive.

If you can learn how to live in the moment, it will allow you to reset your attitude when something bad goes down. Like, if you have a shit call at 8:00 a.m. about the world falling apart, you're then prepared to compartmentalize the emotions attached to that specific circumstance and reboot your mentality for the rest of the day. You can only control what happens next, not what already transpired. A lot of people fall into the trap of living in the past and trying to rewrite history, which is impossible. Let's say a client yells at you about something and you're frustrated about it. What can you do? You can't reverse the conversation or delete what they said. So you have two options. You can either marinate in your own misery and feel sorry for yourself. Or you can transfer your energy to something productive that may make that client feel better in the long run, which will also make your day better. If you lose an account or a listing, what's done is done. There's usually nothing you can do about it. But what you can do is go get a new account or a new listing.

Naturally there are also strategies you can adopt so that negative things don't happen in the first place, in terms of your work ethic and your attention to detail. Sometimes you even have to cut off a toxic client, which is especially hard when they're bringing in a lot of money. One example of this is a very wealthy gentleman who also has a history of being extremely cheap and not wanting to pay commission. In addition to that, according to him, everything always sucks in life. There's a big black cloud that follows him around, and his general feeling is that nobody deserves what they work for. Over the years, I've been hired by him. I've fired him. I've been rehired by him. He's fired me. I've rehired him. And I've refired him. It's been a constant back-and-forth because the commissions from his $20-plus million deals are so massive that I'm always willing to give it another shot. But, finally, it came to a point where I realized no amount of money was worth his negative energy and that the amount of time and attention he required was pulling me away from my other important clients. Our last encounter was so exhausting that I literally gave him back his $20 million listing. I just couldn't manage his toxicity anymore. And, guess what? Within two weeks, I had fresh inventory, I was negotiating new deals, and my mindset had been reset to positive. Once I let it go, all of a sudden the money started to flow again.

This goes to show that, inevitably, there comes a time in everyone's lives when things simply don't go your way, which may or may not be your fault, and you have to effect change. It's like the game of baseball. If a player gets a hit about a third of the time he's up at bat for the length of his career, chances are he'll be in the Hall of Fame. This means that same player got out the other two-thirds of the time. Sounds like a major fail when you think of it that way, yet it's not. He can't do anything about his strikeout or his line drive into the first baseman's glove. It happened. With that said, the next time he gets up to bat, he can hit it past third base or, if he's really lucky, out of the park, which contributes to his overall earned run average. This is why athletes understand that succeeding in sports isn't purely about physical prowess; it has a lot to do with your mental faculties as well. If you obsess over every crappy swing, squandered shot, or missed goal, you won't be able to push forward and overcome those obstacles. As Muhammad Ali, the greatest heavyweight boxer of all time said, "Champions aren't made in the gyms. Champions are made from something they have deep inside them: a desire, a dream, a vision."

THE UNIVERSE POSSESSES ENERGY

It's my personal belief that the world around us possesses energy. If you're religious, you may call that energy God, but whatever name you want to assign to it, it's out there. To further that conviction, I also think that the human mind and body can tap into and control that energy, both positively and negatively.

The way to go about this is to be open-minded and allow yourself to experience different practices, which is something that I didn't understand until about twenty years ago, when I first got into real estate. As I mentioned earlier, Kyle and I were kind of down and out financially during that time, so we decided to go to The Kabbalah Centre in Los Angeles to learn more about their ideology. To give you a sense of what kabbalah is all about, it's an ancient spiritual wisdom that offers practical insights. It's literal meaning is "to receive," and it teaches that every human being was created to receive complete joy and fulfillment. One of the primary principles of kabbalah is that everything has a reason and purpose; there are no coincidences. It asks questions such as: *How can we know we're on the path our soul is meant to take? How can we live a life of purpose and meaning? How do we live joyously? Can we all positively impact others, and thereby, the world?*

If you think about it, it makes a lot of sense that we were put on this earth to find our purpose, to be happy, and to spread love to those around us. I truly wish more people embraced these ideas. When you're inherently content in life, you instinctively want to give to those in need or those who've yet to reach their potential. When you're generous by nature, you're paid back tenfold, though that can't be your intention. Benevolence shouldn't be viewed as an investment. It's not like buying a stock for twenty dollars and making a hundred. It's a mindset. It's your way of mining the universe's energy and sharing your joy and goodwill with your family, your friends and, often—most significantly—with complete strangers.

By incorporating charitable endeavors into your life, you put yourself in a place to receive. And you give yourself peace of mind. Sometimes there's a fiscal reward, even though that's not the objective.

As far as I'm concerned, there's no doubt that my positive mindset has had a major impact on my success. Again, it goes back to the notions of daydreaming and manifesting, which can exist independently or in unison. When you operate from a place of optimism, you can then visualize everything you want in life and spend every day working toward that goal. It doesn't have to be innate. Honestly, I think it's something I've learned over the years and has now become second nature to me.

It's also something that I teach my kids and the agents who work for me. I encourage them to look at things from various angles, until they land on what feels right to them. I love helping people find their purpose, because I know how rewarding that is. But, I will say, if somebody wants to probe me for advice, they need to be prepared and motivated toward something specific. I can't help someone who asks me, "How do I sell a house?" Conversely, if an individual approaches me and says, "I've been prospecting, here's what I'm doing, and I'm not getting any leads. How can I improve?"—then I can walk them through each step.

For example, a number of year ago, a gentleman named John, who was already working for me, came into my office and said, "Mauricio, I'm very frustrated. I'm not as successful as I'd like to be. And I'm beginning to wonder if real estate is for me. How do I become you?"

I replied, "I can't tell you how to be me. You need to find out who you are. Let's set up a thirty-minute session so you can show me what you're doing." We arranged a meeting for two weeks later; he walked into my office and started taking me through his approach, which was one hundred cold calls a day and five hundred cold calls a week.

I pressed him further by asking, "What do you do on those calls?"

And he explained that his primary goal was to get an appointment with the client.

I continued, "Okay, so when you don't get an appointment, you hang up and move on to the next person?"

He nodded and, immediately, I knew what he needed to change. I told him that instead of making one hundred calls a day, he should be making ten calls.

I said, "If you get someone on the phone, consider that your appointment. You don't need to sit with them in person and feed them a whole bunch of bullshit. Before you make each call, I want you to learn everything you can about the person on the other end of the line. What does their house look like? Are the photos online good enough? Is the listing expired?" I watched as John began to understand exactly what had been holding him back. And even though I was the one sharing my time and expertise, that interaction made me feel like I was making a difference in someone else's life. Sure enough, thirty days later, he returned to my office to share that he'd landed three listings. Today, John—a guy who was ready to quit real estate—is one of our top agents. Not because I taught him to be me, which never would have worked. But because I gave him the tools to be his best self.

BE A BELIEVER

When your mindset is in the right place, it opens you up to believing in things that may seem implausible or even otherworldly to those around you. To my point, throughout the years, I showed Michael Jackson numerous homes. Michael was a friend of Kyle's, and he had one of the most beautiful, ethereal voices of anyone I've ever known. There were times when I'd be showing him a property and the home would have fantastic acoustics, so he'd start singing a cappella right on the spot. It was incredible to hear.

When Michael passed away, he was leasing a house on Carolwood in Holmby Hills, and I was hired by the owner to sell it. Michael had actually died in the secondary master bedroom and—by the time I got to it—no one was living there, so I was taking care of the place.

One of the things I pride myself on and that I've taught everyone who works for me is that when you're given the keys to a home you're selling, you have to treat it like it's your house. This means you have to turn everything off when you leave, make sure all the doors are locked and the windows are closed, and then you have to take the keys with you. It's one of the basic rules of real estate.

I learned this the hard way when I got a spectacular listing in Malibu from a new and very wealthy client—someone I was extremely excited to work with. One day when I was leaving the house, I had back-to-back meetings, and I was in a hurry. As a result, I didn't secure the house properly and the windows were left open. It was a real rookie mistake, not to mention a very costly one. Two days later, I got a call from the client, who was understandably livid because seagulls had infiltrated his home and they'd shit all over the place, so much so that the interior was ruined. Needless to say, I lost the listing, and I lost the client. After that, I vowed never to screw up in that way again—and definitely not for Michael Jackson, a man I had and still have endless respect for.

You can imagine how many people wanted to see his house, especially since it was where he'd passed away. Even though there was an extensive vetting process to determine which clients were serious about buying the home and which ones were merely fans looking to satisfy their morbid curiosity, there were still a lot of showings. So, every night, I'd leave the house late and return early the following morning. As I mentioned, Michael died in the secondary master bedroom, which

had an amazing stereo and windows that faced the back gar-
den. Apparently, he used to listen to music and stare out those
windows; it was his favorite spot in the house.

One morning, when I walked into that bedroom, the stereo was on and the window was open. I was like, *What the hell
is going on here?* I was completely freaked out, because I was
absolutely positive that I'd turned off the stereo and closed the
window the night before. The only conceivable answer was
that Michael's spirit had been there, but I was still questioning
whether I'd been thorough enough.

That evening when I left the house, I checked the stereo,
the window, and all the lights what felt like fifty times! The
next day, I came back and the lights were on, music was playing, and the window was open *again*. Immediately, I called
the owner to double-check that no one had been there. He
confirmed that not one person had set foot in the home since
I'd locked up.

If that wasn't enough to convince me that Michael's ghost
had been present, when the time came to go into escrow and
do the final walk-through of the property with the buyer, he
discovered that the switch that controlled this huge chandelier
in the foyer was broken. It was supposed to move the chandelier up and down, and it wasn't working.

He said, "I'm not closing on the house until it's fixed."

I told him it was kind of ridiculous to blow up the whole
deal over a three-horsepower motor. I mean, give me a break.

But, no matter how many ways I tried to convince him otherwise, he stood firm, and I was totally annoyed.

As the buyer meandered into another room, I literally looked up toward the sky—as a last-ditch effort—and said, "Michael, please help me out here." Then I walked back over to the switch and, by some miracle, the chandelier started going up and down. It was working perfectly. The client came back in and began playing with the switch, as if he wanted to break it again, but he couldn't.

I looked at him, smiled, and said, "Looks like we're closing after all." And then I said a silent thank-you to Michael Jackson.

SINK OR SWIM

A key element to maintaining a positive attitude in life and business is surrounding yourself with well-intentioned individuals and encouraging them to spread their wings. When I'm looking to hire someone, I rely heavily on my gut instinct. In part because I have an uncanny ability to recognize authenticity and also to smell bullshit. But also because I like to give people the chance to sink or swim. I'm not someone who spends a lot of time hemming and hawing over these kinds of decisions. My philosophy is usually: What's the worst that can happen? I'll meet with a prospective employee for fifteen minutes and, if I'm impressed by them, I'll offer them a job. My feeling is that there's no real way to know how they're going to perform until they're actually in the position. Conversely, when Billy Rose hired his assistant, he studied 250 résumés and asked fifty candidates to take a personality assessment. Then he interviewed around ten of them; it was a whole thing. I don't formally test anyone. My viewpoint is that you have to let people try and they'll either succeed or learn from their mistakes. There's always an opportunity for growth where I'm concerned.

This doesn't mean I haven't made mistakes. For instance, The Agency jumped very quickly into partnerships in Arizona and Florida that didn't pan out the way we had hoped, which was unfortunate. So, what did we do? We stepped in, fixed the boat, and got it to start sailing again.

The story with Arizona, in my opinion, is that, unfortunately, the business wasn't succeeding under the leadership of the people we'd joined forces with. It wasn't easy, because despite the failure, they were good salespeople and we'd really tried to make it work. Since they owned 50 percent and we owned 50 percent, we had to unwind the partnership agreement, take back their half, and turn it into a 100 percent corporate-owned office, which it is today. The reality is that sometimes you just have to accept the loss or the poor decision and effect change.

In Florida, to my mind, we created a similar fifty-fifty partnership with two people and created a hybrid of a franchise scenario, which was not successful, because it meant that we were on both sides of the deal. Additionally, as I recall, there was some deceitful behavior involved, so we had to go back and unravel that affiliation.

Out of seventy offices, we've had two missteps, which is not a bad mathematical percentage. From my perspective, if something doesn't work, giving up isn't an option. I'll either find a way to remedy the situation or come at it from a different angle. If, for some reason, the situation is completely unwinnable, I'll change my course of action entirely. It goes back to possessing the confidence to know that you can figure out a way to succeed, despite any and all hurdles in your way.

I like to think of my approach as taking calculated risks. I'm not about to put my life's savings in jeopardy, but I am willing to gamble to a certain degree. And while I do believe that following an innate reflex can be beneficial, especially when you trust yourself and your track record, I'd never embolden someone to pursue something that would seriously threaten their financial well-being. That's where the calculated part comes in. You can only act like a cowboy when you can afford to be one. For this reason, I never enter into a deal or partnership without understanding the economic parameters—namely what I stand to gain if things go well and what I stand to lose if they don't.

In addition to hiring individuals who share my positive posture, I also prefer to employ people who have explicit opinions. One of the most important things I look for when interviewing applicants is their ability to think on their own and that they do so in an intelligent manner. I don't have to agree with their ideas, but as long as I can wrap my head around them and embrace their vision, I'm cool with that. Everyone's brain operates in a unique way, and that's something that intrigues me. As a boss, it's vital to support that ingenuity, regardless of whether you understand it. You never know what you might learn from someone, even if they do have less experience.

I tell everybody who works for me, "I have zero interest in you conveying what you think I want to hear. Or echoing the same things I'm saying to you. I want to know your thoughts about a particular circumstance or problem." I ask my employees questions like, *How can we better market ourselves? Should we be courting more agents or laying off to save money? What's been effective for us and what hasn't been?* I may or may not agree with their answers, and—in the end—I'll make my own decision, which I'll live and die by, but I listen first. I heed their advice. That's why they have a job at The Agency. To communicate what they know and what they believe, without worrying about what I know and believe. If you run your company like a tyrant with little or no respect for the comprehension of your staff, then you're doing yourself a disservice. And, suddenly, your positive environment has turned negative.

I expect people to make mistakes. As strange as it may sound, I want them to. You can't create, innovate, or progress if you're not willing to take risks. And if you're not willing to take risks and you're not willing to disagree with me or deviate from the status quo, I don't want you working for us.

TAKE PRIDE IN YOUR TEAM

Two of the best people I've ever hired, both of whom I have tremendous admiration for, are Santiago Arana and Mike Leipart (whom I spoke briefly about in chapter 4).

Santiago is a principal and partner—he's ranked the number six real estate agent in the country and has closed billions of dollars in deals across Los Angeles.

He hails from Bolivia, and his success story truly represents the American dream. He arrived in the United States with no money to his name and only spoke Spanish. He worked first as a busboy and then as a waiter at two very high-end restaurants, one in Los Angeles called L'Orangerie and another in Santa Barbara called Cava. He used to see customers come in and drop thousands of dollars on wine and champagne, which motivated him to make something of himself. So he learned to speak English and subsequently got into real estate before I met him a little over a decade ago. At the time, he was working for Sotheby's, but the second I met him, I felt an immediate connection, and I knew he would be an unbelievable asset to our team. In 2014, he joined The Agency and has since become like a younger brother to me and also a respected confidant. What

I love about Santiago is that he's incredibly driven, passionate, and also very spiritual. He's actually taught me so much about meditation and how to maintain a positive mindset.

About a year after we hired him, I remember saying, "Santee, you're going to be one of the top Realtors in the country. One day, you're going to beat me. But I'm not going to make it easy for you. You're going to have to fight hard."

Two years ago, he beat me for the first time in volume and became our number one agent. He heads our office in Brentwood and is now my partner in Miami as well. Santiago has been a true inspiration to me in every way.

Mike Leipart, our managing partner of The Agency Development Group, is another instrumental asset to our team and someone who's also a very positive force for me. His role is to guide developers of luxury properties worldwide through every stage of the process, from preconstruction design input to sales operation oversight. I largely credit him for The Agency becoming the only West Coast–based organization to merge the knowledge and experience of a residential real estate brokerage with the proficiency of a dedicated development marketing and strategic sales planning team.

He came into my life as we were starting The Agency, while he was the senior vice president and national marketing director at ST Residential. Part of Mike's job there was to put together teams to sell apartment buildings across the country. Through this, he began to realize that when something went wrong, all of the individuals who worked on these projects would blame one another. There wasn't one company that had a complete solution with creative, sales, marketing, and research under one roof—so that finger-pointing wouldn't be an issue.

As soon as I met Mike, I realized how smart he was, and, once we'd met a few times, I told him that we were launching a new-development division at The Agency and I asked him to consult for us on the side. I was fascinated by his ideas and everything he'd learned in his position at ST Residential, and he really shared that knowledge and energy with us and helped guide us in conceptualizing the division.

Eventually, he ended up getting fired from ST, which goes back to my theory that when one door closes, another better door often opens, and we seized the opportunity to ask him to come work for The Agency full-time and officially head up our new-development division. We really valued each other's philosophies and I especially appreciated that his brain works so differently than anybody else's, including mine. So he moved his family from Oklahoma to Los Angeles and joined our team.

What continues to amaze me about Mike is that he's a guy who wears a million hats and he intellectualizes things in such a unique way, which allows me to bounce ideas off him. He's opened my mind to so many various perspectives.

I'll never forget how when he first started working for us, I was asking his opinion on something, and he said to me, "Mauricio, what you want to hear is XYZ."

And I replied, "Mike, if you ever tell me what I want to hear, you won't do me any good. I hired you because I like your brain. I want to hear what you want to tell me and what you think of things. That doesn't mean I'm going to listen to you every time or follow your advice, but that's what I'm interested in."

Over the years, not only has Mike been one of the strongest members of our team, but he's become a very good friend. His wife is also one of Kyle's best friends, and his daughter and my daughter Portia are super close as well.

It's people like Mike and Santiago who allow me to keep my head on straight and continue to grow both professionally and personally.

FORGIVE AND FORGET

Another significant aspect of leading with positivity is the ability to forgive faults, slipups, and oversights and truly leave them in the past. A couple of years ago, my assistant, Jane, made a pretty big mistake, one that cost The Agency about $35,000. She was handling the furniture inventory for a home we were representing and had sent the buyer's agent five pages of photos of the items our clients were keeping. When the buyer's agent sent her back only four blurry scanned pages with his clients' approval, Jane didn't realize they'd removed one entire page and simply used her original copy to mark the edits they'd made. This meant that only a few pieces of furniture were omitted rather than the whole missing page, which the buyer assumed they could keep. Soon enough, Jane realized her error, called the buyer's agent, and said, "Hey, I messed up. Can you please let your clients know that page five is not included?"

The agent's reply was swift and firm: "Absolutely not. We're only moving along with this deal because they want that stuff."

Jane knew she'd massively screwed up and that she had to admit it. She came to me directly, confessed her wrongdoing, apologized profusely, and said it would never happen again. Since Jane had already proved herself as a competent and loyal assistant, my response was, "Well, I guess I'll have to pay for the furniture." Not for one minute did I make her feel like shit about it. And I definitely didn't throw it back in her face at a later date. That kind of behavior breeds a hostile work environment.

When you're in a position of authority, you have to realize that nobody's perfect. God knows I've made a lot of mistakes in my life. So, even though Jane is tremendously skilled, there's no way she's going to bat a thousand. With that said, I did take the opportunity to make sure she understood that she'd screwed up and that it was going to cost us a chunk of change to remedy the situation. Trust me, she's never forgotten that moment. Of course if someone continues to be careless, you can't forgive them repeatedly, but if it's a one-off lapse, the prospect of teaching someone how to learn from their error and move on is far more valuable than punishing them for being human.

RIGHT YOUR WRONGS

Upholding an affirmative mindset is as important in your personal life as it is on the work front. I'm truly lucky to have such wonderful, positive relationships with everyone in my family, but it wasn't always that way with my sister, Sharon. To be blunt, as the older brother, I was a total asshole to her. Because of my various struggles in childhood, my parents paid much more attention to me and it seemed to me that I was the favorite, which meant I would push the boundaries and get away with all sorts of shit that Sharon couldn't. In turn, my sister was so caring and attentive to me. She loved me more than anything in the entire world. And, remarkably, she put up with my crap without complaint.

It wasn't until I was in my twenties, when we were both working for our father's textiles company, that I fully grasped the error of my ways. Suddenly, we were on an equal playing field, and I saw Sharon in a whole new light. I'd always known she was a smart, fundamentally good person, but I'd never given her the credit where it was due. After that, she joined me at 90265 and ran all of our production, which was when our relationship started to change for the better. Still, on the personal side, we weren't as close as I wanted us to be. I realized this was my fault and that if I wanted to mend things, I had to alter my mindset and put in the effort.

My first real opportunity to make that happen was when Sharon and I both got married and started having kids. In many ways, I have Kyle to thank for that, because she taught me how to be a more compassionate person and how to possess the humility it takes to show someone you love that they're important to you. With Kyle's guidance and by becoming a father to four daughters, I became increasingly in touch with my feminine side, which allowed me to feel complete both mentally and emotionally. It also allowed me to be a better brother to Sharon.

Now, my sister works at The Agency, and even though she and her husband, two sons, and a daughter—all of whom I adore—live a little under an hour away from us, we try to see each other socially as often as we can.

Above all, acknowledging my past errors and the fact that I didn't treat Sharon the way she deserved to be treated, has made me a better man.

NO NEED FOR GREED

On the flip side, one of the easiest ways to fall into a negative mindset is by being greedy. I'll go so far as to say it's among the worst traits a human being can possess, especially in the professional arena. This goes for anyone in any business, but I see it a lot with real estate developers, and I've probably sold more homes for developers than anybody I know. If a developer becomes greedy, it almost always leads to bankruptcy. For some reason developers feel like they're not allowed to lose money on homes they build and invest in. Oddly, they do seem to understand that if they buy, for example, Facebook stock at $100 and they want to liquidate it at $70, they're going to lose money. Yet if they spend $5 million on a house and its value drops to $4.5 million, they refuse to accept the loss. The thing is, market conditions dictate the value of your asset, period, end of story. Right before the 2007 recession, I had one developer who'd invested $8 million to build a home. And I got him an $11.5 million offer, which was great.

He said to me, "Mauricio, I need twelve million."

I replied, "I'm sorry to tell you this, but that's not a smart decision."

And he countered, "It's an ego thing. I have to hit that mark."

I was like, "Brother, I promise you, you're never going to see this offer again. Don't be stupid." I begged him to take it. But, at the end of the day, he didn't. Three months later, the recession hit and the market dropped by 30 percent. This developer ended up forfeiting the house to the bank. Unfortunately, this story happens over and over again.

MAURICIO'S MANTRAS

- When you love what you do, and it's something you're truly passionate about, you're always going to have the best day.

- The universe possesses energy, and the human mind and body can tap into and control that energy, both positively and negatively.

- If you run your company like a tyrant with little or no respect for the comprehension of your staff, then you're doing yourself a disservice. And, suddenly, your positive environment has turned negative.

- When your mindset is in the right place, it opens you up to believing in things that may seem implausible or even otherworldly to those around you.

- You can't create, innovate, or progress if you're not willing to take risks.

- When you take pride in your team, they'll help you grow both professionally and personally.

- When you're in a position of authority, you have to realize that nobody's perfect. The opportunity to teach someone how to learn from their mistake and move on is far more valuable than punishing them for being human.

- One of the key elements to maintaining a positive attitude in business is surrounding yourself with good people and encouraging them to spread their wings.

- Upholding an affirmative mindset is as important in your personal life as it is on the work front and acknowledging your past errors will make you a better person.

- One of the easiest ways to fall into a negative mindset is by being greedy. It's among the worst traits a human being can possess, especially in the professional arena.

CHAPTER 9

BALANCING ACT

Most of us spend too much time on what is urgent
and not enough time on what is important.

–Stephen R. Covey, bestselling author
of *The 7 Habits of Highly Effective People*

CURATE YOUR LIFESTYLE

In the introduction to this book, I wrote that my grandfather used to tell me there are twenty-four hours in a day—eight for sleep, eight for work, and eight for play—and that it's up to me to decide how to use those hours wisely. As I've heeded this advice throughout the years, my experience has been that when you can create a balance between these three elements, it will lead to sanity and longevity at work and will allow you to keep the spark alive between you and your partner. This means that I attempt to get a full night's sleep whenever possible. It also means that when I'm working, my goal is to focus all of my energy on getting the job done, and when I'm playing—whether it's hanging out with my family, exercising, skiing, or golfing—I'll try to set my phone aside to limit distractions. Of course, there are case-by-case exceptions to this rule, certainly in the event of an emergency or when I determine there's an urgent professional situation I can't ignore, but overall, achieving relative equilibrium in your life is one of the healthiest things you can do for yourself.

As with anything, creating balance is easier said than done, especially when you're working hard, you've got a family that needs you and wants to be with you, and you want to carve out time for yourself. In my opinion, time is the most precious commodity in the world, so I'm very particular about how I use it. This includes maintaining a tight schedule. Every day, I look at my calendar in either thirty-minute or one-hour blocks. And then I ask myself how I can maximize my productivity during those blocks. For example, can I do six five-minute calls? Or is one call going to take me a full half hour?

I believe the first and most important aspect of balance is efficiency. When you're efficient, you get the most out of the time you have. The second thing goes back to the concept of a healthy mindset, which allows you to be as resourceful and prolific as possible. In order to preserve a healthy mindset, you need to find those hours to do things you enjoy and to be with your loved ones, whatever that looks like for you. Maybe it's having lunch with a friend, going to a concert with your partner, or driving your kids to school. It could also be something as simple as meditating. I know that when I meditate for even twenty minutes, time seems to stand still, and those twenty minutes can provide me with the same amount of peace as three hours of being a couch potato, which is not my thing.

Unfortunately, from my perspective—because I'm a very busy person—there are never enough hours in the day for everything I'd like to do. So, as someone who's always being pulled in multiple directions, you have to learn to sacrifice certain things. One of the sacrifices I've had to make is hanging out with good friends, which is something that's important to me. My schedule just doesn't allow for a three-hour lunch on a Friday. And I do have friends who have forty Friday lunches a year, whereas I can squeeze in maybe six to eight, if I'm lucky.

When you have a career in real estate, you're working seven days a week, certainly in the beginning. There are always open houses on the weekends and clients who want to see homes on Saturdays and Sundays. As a result of this, through the years, I also had to forgo time with my kids. One big sacrifice I made was not being a soccer dad. I wanted more than anything to coach my daughter's AYSO (American Youth Soccer Organization) team, but because of my commitment to my career at a period in my life when I needed to make money, I couldn't do that. Missing out on this is a definite regret in my life. There's nothing I can do about it except acknowledge it. Everyone has regrets, and it's pointless to pretend otherwise. When you recognize these disappointments and realize that you can never go backward and erase things that have already happened, it allows you to be a better human being moving forward.

In the way of self-time, you have to make it happen. If you don't, you'll become unhealthy. This may involve changing your own schedule to accommodate other priorities. In my case, I love to play golf. So, in order to make that work, I tee off on Saturdays and Sundays at 6:00 a.m. By doing that, I extend my own day. Sure, I have to wake up earlier, which may mean I get seven hours of sleep instead of the coveted eight, but then I'm off the course by 10:00 a.m., and I can either be showing properties by ten thirty or back home swimming and having lunch with Kyle and my girls. I know a lot of people who don't get up until 10:00 or 11:00 a.m. on the weekends, which is fine on occasion—when you really need some relaxation or downtime—but if you're sleeping in regularly, you're not maximizing your life. Instead, you're wasting hours you'll never get back.

YIN AND YANG

While thoughtful time management is essential to attaining balance, so is finding a significant other who complements you and supports you. This can be especially challenging when you're with someone who also has a big career. For example, Kyle works really hard too, but she always makes sure that the kids and I come home to a welcoming atmosphere. She has candles lit, soothing music on, and ambient lighting, so that when I walk in the door after a long day, I feel happy and loved.

If I came home, as many people I know do, and all the lights were off and my wife was in her pajamas under the covers, it would feel like my day was over, which isn't what I need and want. If one of us is working until, say, 8:30 p.m., we wait for the other one to have dinner. We've never been a family—even when our kids were younger—where the kids ate before us. That quality time, sharing a meal together, is a fundamental part of our balance. Otherwise, if the kids were done eating at six thirty and then they went to bed a couple of hours later, all of a sudden I wouldn't have any time with them and they wouldn't get to see me at all.

In any relationship and family, there has to be a yin and a yang, so that you can find the ideal balance for everyone. It's all about respecting each other and, obviously, having fun. What I mean by that is laughing with each other and sharing and being open. Very few people talk about how important mindset is for relationships; we always talk about mindset for self, but both are equally necessary. If you're not happy together, then what's life all about?

My favorite thing about Kyle is her sense of humor and her ability to make me laugh. I don't know if there's anything better than that in the world. Clearly, she's gorgeous, but that's just the surface. She's also beautiful on the inside.

For my part, I try to be sensitive to her needs, emotionally available, and also responsible when it comes to the things she depends on me for. This includes respecting each other's personal space and also being mentally and physically present. If one person in the couple is just working, working, working, and then has a whole bunch of guys' or girls' nights and trips, that does not lead to a successful partnership.

I'm not going to lie, it definitely takes some serious finessing and flexibility to make it work, but you just have to do the best you can. As I said, in addition to my demanding schedule, Kyle has been on *The Real Housewives of Beverly Hills* for twelve years, and I have too in some capacity.

Each season has been very different in the way of my commitment. The husbands played a much bigger role in seasons one and two, even into season three. Back then we were invited on the yearly trip with the women, but as time passed, they stopped doing that.

Honestly, I love being on the show—it's fun for me, because it's not something I have to do. I don't get paid for it; I'm just there as Kyle's husband. And that's not at all a complaint. I've never wanted to be compensated or asked to be, which is very intentional. I do it to support my wife and also because I'm well aware of what the show has done for our family in terms of visibility and professional growth. With that said, in any given moment, if I have to choose between filming a scene for *RHOBH* or getting something done for The Agency, the latter always comes first, which Kyle completely understands.

In addition to our busy careers, we also have four daughters, who all required and deserved our attention through the years. Every day was different, yet we always found a way to get through. When the girls were growing up, we lived right near their school, so Kyle and I (or one of us, depending on what else was going on) would walk them to school before heading to work. Then Kyle would figure out how to pick them up. That time walking them to school, or even driving them on occasion, was irreplaceable. Whether we were singing along with the radio or I was getting some cool gossip, I needed that, and so did they. If for some reason I had a conference call and couldn't talk to them for those few minutes, it gave me a lot of anxiety and altered my mood. Obviously, there were circumstances where I had no choice, but I didn't like it.

I truly believe that if you can be transparent and collaborative with the people you love, then you can create a positive environment for everyone in your family. You have to invest the same amount of energy into your personal life as you do into your career in order to foster a culture of respect. When you do that, your significant other and your kids will understand that sometimes sacrifices need to be made, but they'll also be proud of you and everything you've accomplished.

KEEP AN OPEN DIALOGUE

Expanding on the idea of transparency, another major aspect of balance is keeping an open dialogue with your kids, and this is also one of the hardest things on earth to manage. As a parent, instinctively, you want to tell your kids what to do because you've done it and you know what's right and what's wrong. By the same token, if you think back to when you were a child and your parents told you what to do, you had so much resentment toward them! You and your partner need to develop a game plan for how to approach child-rearing in a way that works for everyone.

In my marriage, Kyle is the rule maker. She's the one who punishes the kids when they do something out of turn or don't listen. And I support that 100 percent. Conversely, my method of parenting is to lead by example and to ask questions and try to get my kids to arrive at the same conclusion I've already arrived at. By encouraging them to provide answers, I lead them to understand the error of their ways on their own, which I find to be effective most of the time.

Although I definitely parent through fear as well. Take this whole fentanyl craze as an example. My daughter Portia is only fifteen years old. I've told her repeatedly that, down the line, if she ever gets handed fentanyl or any other drug, it's bad news. I will literally scare her by saying, "What if you're at a party and you've smoked a little joint or had some alcohol and you're impaired and somebody hands you an ecstasy pill that you don't even know is an ecstasy pill and you take it and it's got fentanyl in it? Guess what? Because of that wrong decision— you could die. Think about that."

In the same conversation, I'll convey to Portia (and this has always gone for any of my daughters) that everyone makes stupid mistakes. And that if they're ever outside the house and need help, or if they need me to come and pick them up at three o'clock in the morning, they should absolutely call me immediately. I say, "As long as you reach out to me, I promise you will not get a lesson, there will not be any questions asked. I will be fucking thrilled. And, by the way, I might be in a bad mood because you woke me up. But I'll get you home safely, without judgment."

I think a lot of parents make the mistake of condemning their kids for not being an extension of them. They try to mold them to be replicas. But everyone is different. You have to raise your children to be independent thinkers, while providing them with a moral compass and teaching them to make smart decisions. If you can do that, you will be extraordinarily successful.

A few months ago, I went on a hike with my daughter Alexia. We were chatting casually about life and whether she was happy with things like her current romantic relationship. I let her talk, and I listened. I'm never one to force a conversation with my kids, and I don't like to offer strong advice, because—at this point—my feeling is that Kyle and I have given our girls the right foundation so they can figure out what's right and wrong on their own.

Over the years, they've definitely dated people I wasn't thrilled about, but my approach has always been to let it play out. I'm not the one in the relationship, so I believe it's up to them to decide whether to stay with someone. In every one of these cases, they've made their own decisions and ultimately broken up with the person, which is way better than if I'd tried to cause it. Although I've definitely made my opinion known after the fact!

The only piece of wisdom I've shared with my daughters is to find the person who checks all of their boxes and feels right to them. I make it clear that they can talk to me about anything. But, again, I allow them to make their own choices with the understanding that my guidance is available if they need it or want it. That is how you achieve balance as a parent.

WORKING WITH FAMILY

Combining the professional and personal areas of your life can definitely be tricky. I know this firsthand, since I currently work with my father, my sister, and two of my daughters. So, at The Agency, not only am I the CEO, but I'm a son, a brother, and a father. And I love every minute of it.

Though I will say that I never pushed my daughters to join the firm. I've always told them it was an available opportunity for them, without any pressure. When Farrah was finishing up college, she knew she wanted to come work with me, because she's always been interested in real estate. She actually started as my assistant while I was still at Hilton & Hyland and only dealing with sales. It was such a stellar experience for her because I had a lot more time back then than I do now, so I was able to train her and really help her understand the business. She shadowed me at my listings, learned, and listened. She was a total sponge, absorbing all the ins and outs of the business, including how to negotiate and manage contracts.

As for Alexia, once she'd finished college, she also decided to join The Agency completely on her own. Neither Farrah nor I influenced that choice, but she's an absolute natural and really coming into her own.

Sophia just graduated from George Washington University. She didn't confirm her career path at first but just recently she decided to come to The Agency as well. There's actually a scene at the end of the first season of *Buying Beverly Hills* where we tease that prospect. I'm not going to lie, I'm thrilled to have all three of them working with me, but I would have been equally delighted if any of them had chosen to pursue other interests.

One of the best parts of my life is the ability to work with my kids and to get to know them on a professional level. I'm very careful not to give them preferential treatment. In fact, sometimes I think I make it a little bit more difficult so that there's not even a hint of nepotism where they're concerned.

On any given day, we have all three generations together at the office. It's such a gift to watch the relationship between my father and his grandkids. And also my sister and her nieces.

Where it gets complicated is that my family members want to be able to reach me whenever they need to, and they expect me to be there for them in those moments. The thing is, I have sixteen hundred employees right now. I'm running a huge company. This means that there are inevitably going to be things that I can't deliver on, certainly not immediately. And I have to prioritize and set boundaries, while being considerate of the fact that my family is extremely important to me. The best and only way to do this is by communicating and collaborating, so that no one feels diminished or rejected.

Let's say my sister is selling a property and needs an answer from me immediately but I'm in a meeting. I'll explain to her that I'm happy to speak to her later in the day and that we will resolve her issue but that I'm tied up and can't abandon whatever I'm working on just because she wants to reach me. Nine times out of ten, people appreciate when you're direct with them and set expectations appropriately.

There are also plenty of occasions when Farrah and Alexia will want to discuss one of their deals when we're at home, because they know they have my undivided attention. I get that, but I'm cautious not to let work consume my personal time or theirs. None of my other agents get to chat about their clients or transactions at the dinner table, so that's a situation where boundaries come into play.

I try to put myself in their position. How would I react if I needed something from them and they weren't available? What would that feel like? And how would I want them to treat me?

Of course, it's not black-and-white. When you work with family, there are many shades of gray and plenty of instances where your job and your private life bleed into each other, but as long as you're aware of this and careful about protecting your own personal space, it can also be extremely rewarding. There's nothing I love more than watching my family members excel for our company. It gives me immense pride to know that they're passionate about what they do and that we're all in it together in pursuit of a common goal.

SET BOUNDARIES

The concept of setting boundaries to attain balance extends to your career as well. The thing about being a CEO and a real estate agent is that you're constantly dealing with people telling you *there's a fire*. It used to be that when someone who worked for me said the "world was burning to the ground," I'd jump into action and set aside whatever it was I was doing in order to attend to the situation. As I've grown into my role as a leader, I'm more comfortable not replying instantly and not running toward the fire unless I truly believe it's an emergency. I've become much better at taking a beat and dealing with it when the time is right for me.

In order to grow a company successfully, you have to promote a culture where the people who work for you are empowered to fix things on their own. You have to encourage them to think on their feet and let them make mistakes. Every mistake is not necessarily a catastrophe. In fact, it will likely be a teachable moment.

So, if it's a Friday afternoon, and I'm on the golf course, my phone might be blowing up with people who believe that I'm the only one who can solve their problem. But, if I set boundaries effectively and don't answer those texts and calls immediately, I know they'll find a way to solve the issues on their own. By doing this, you will ensure that you don't become a slave to your job and you'll be able to maintain a healthy business environment and a healthy mindset for yourself, which is what I'm all about.

GIVE BACK

I've been very blessed in my life to have a successful career and a loving family—including a significant other who supports me unconditionally and four phenomenal daughters whom I have outstanding and unique relationships with. I'm endlessly grateful for my prosperity, both at work and at home.

In order to create balance in this way, it's extremely important to me to pay it forward and to give back to those less fortunate than I am. Personally, because I grew up with neutropenia, I support Children's Hospital Los Angeles. It's a cause that's near and dear to my heart. For my wife, Kyle, breast cancer awareness is something she champions in a big way, since her mother died from the disease, as a result of not doing regular checks. You don't necessarily have to donate to charities that have had a direct impact on your family, but I think that when this is the case, it allows you to feel more attached to the cause and, therefore, makes you devote that much more time and energy to it.

To that end, on the professional front, The Agency partners with Habitat for Humanity through an organization called Giveback Homes, which is a community of individuals in the real estate industry who create social change by helping build homes for deserving families around the world. I'm actually on the board. It's very important to me that there's a culture of philanthropy prevalent in our company. And that doesn't mean simply buying tickets or a table at an event. Very often, when one of our agents closes a deal on a property, they donate money on behalf of their clients to either Habitat for Humanity or Giveback Homes.

We've also created what we call "build days" where we not only raise money but also roll up our sleeves and help build a home in our community. Since we have offices across the globe, we've been able to offer support in many different areas. Typically, we even have the opportunity to meet the homeowner who's going to be the recipient of the house we're constructing, which is very cool. Our team in Toronto just completed a build day, which they said was extraordinary because they got to help a family in need, see their hard work materialize right before them, and also because it was a true bonding experience to engage in that kind of physical activity with their colleagues. When you give back to others, especially those less privileged than you are, it's a beautiful thing and something we really care about.

MAURICIO'S MANTRAS

- Creating a balance between work, play, and rest will lead to sanity and longevity in your career and will allow you to keep the spark alive with your significant other.

- Look for a partner who complements you, supports you, and challenges you.

- I truly believe that if you can be transparent and collaborative with the people you love, then you can create a positive environment for everyone in your family. You have to invest the same amount of energy into your personal life as you do into your career in order to foster a culture of respect.

- Keeping an open dialogue with your children is so important. If you listen to them, instill them with good morals, and teach them to make smart decisions, you will be an extraordinarily successful parent.

- When working with family, you have to set expectations and communicate effectively.

- As a business owner, you have to create boundaries so that you're not putting out every fire. This means empowering your employees to make decisions and find solutions on their own.

- You don't necessarily have to donate to charities that have had a direct impact on your life, but I think that when this is the case, it allows you to feel more attached to the cause and, therefore, makes you devote that much more time and energy to it.

CHAPTER 10

STAY TRUE TO YOURSELF

To be yourself in a world that is constantly trying
to make you something else is the greatest
accomplishment.

—Ralph Waldo Emerson, American essayist,
philosopher, and poet

NEVER CHANGE WHO YOU ARE

Twelve-plus years ago, when Bravo decided to add *The Real Housewives of Beverly Hills* to the franchise, Kyle was actually the first one cast. From there, she and I brought in Lisa Vanderpump, Adrienne Maloof, and Camille Grammer, who were all clients of mine.

Kyle was no stranger to being on the big or small screen due to her lifelong acting career, but we knew that a reality series would be a very different beast. For this reason, we talked extensively about what it would look like for our family to be featured on the show. Even though it wasn't necessarily something Kyle was looking to pursue, she always wanted to work, and—as I've mentioned before—I never wanted to hold her back in her career. We actually had a fun conversation weighing the pros and cons of exposing ourselves in that way. We considered whether there could be a negative impact on either of our careers, but ultimately came to the conclusion that it would be a great platform for all of us. Honestly, we really didn't spend too much time contemplating. Once we'd given it some thought, we quickly just went for it. I'm a big believer in certainty versus doubt. Once I've evaluated a situation and made a decision, I don't second-guess it. If you're constantly doubting yourself, you can't deliver with excellence, because you'll always be taking two steps forward and one step back.

Of course, being on a reality TV series has not been without its complexities. When you're an actor, you're playing a role, and viewers see you as that character. Let's say it's your job to portray a mass murderer, no one's going to hate you for that, because they realize that you're being paid to depict someone fictional. With unscripted shows, the audience feels like they know you personally, for better and for worse. So when you're on camera sharing everything about yourself, if people hate you on TV, they hate you in real life.

Unfortunately, a lot of people don't think about this. When they're presented with the opportunity to be "famous," it's so enticing that they have to jump on it. They don't consider whether they have skeletons in their closet—as in, maybe they've committed some kind of financial fraud or were abusive in a past relationship—that will be revealed and how that will impact both them and, in many cases, their children. In order to be on reality TV, you have to develop a thick skin and comprehend that there will be negativity that comes with it, no matter who you are or what you've done.

In addition to the actual skeletons, both people who watch the show and the media will invent stuff about you that's not true. They'll also take situations that are perfectly innocuous and turn them into something damaging or simply false. And it can be difficult not to let it get to you.

Thankfully, Kyle and I have always had a very strong marriage. We've been able to stay true to ourselves and not let the hearsay impact our lives or our relationship with each other. I'm very proud of that, because when we started the show, Portia was two, Sophia was ten, and Alexia was fourteen. Those are extremely impressionable ages, especially for girls, and they essentially grew up with cameras in their faces, which is tough. I will say, though, that there was never a time when they came to us and asked not to be seen and they never had issues with the other kids at school. They've always been so well-adjusted, and we're grateful for that.

I believe that one of the reasons for this is that Kyle has always seen her role on *The Real Housewives* as a job, which it is. Unlike many other cast members, when the camera crew leaves our house, we almost never talk about the story lines or what's happening on the show. And we definitely don't focus on how to promote ourselves or create more business for ourselves during family time. We may discuss those types of things during working hours, like if we want to launch a clothing line or something similar, but that's absolutely not the topic of our conversation at the dinner table. The same goes for my new show *Buying Beverly Hills* on Netflix, which I star in with my father, my sister, and two of my daughters—Farrah and Alexia. What happens during filming stays there.

The funny thing is that, sometimes, I actually forget I'm on TV and that people recognize me, even after a decade-plus on the air. I don't know how or why, but it truly hasn't gone to my head or Kyle's or our kids', which is so healthy. Honestly, there are occasions where I'll be talking to someone at a restaurant or in a store, it could be a valet parking attendant or a limo driver, and I have no recollection of the fact that I'm in the public spotlight. All of a sudden, a random stranger will come up to me and say, "Hey, Mauricio, can I have a photo with you?" And for a moment I'm surprised. I'm like, *Oh yeah, I forgot that a lot of people know who I am.*

From a mindset perspective, that's so important. You have to be confident in who you are as a person and not change that for anyone. Kyle and I, and our kids, were built a certain way and just because we're on television doesn't mean we deserve special treatment or should be more empowered than others to get what we want. I see so many people, specifically on reality shows, who feel entitled because they believe they're a celebrity. And I think to myself, *Who cares?* It's a job. Plain and simple. You're no better than anyone else.

I will say that one of the nice things about being on television is that it gives you a platform to do good in the world and, also, to teach people in a positive way. For example, my hope is that the lessons in this book will help readers improve their lives. If it changes even one thing for one person for the better, all the crap that comes with being "famous" is so worth it.

FAME AND FRIENDSHIP

The thing about reality television is that, even when you're true to who you are, it undoubtedly puts friendships to the test. Sometimes it can be destructive and in the best of circumstances it can help build strong, enduring bonds.

The reason for this is that these women are thrust together in a very intense environment. And when you have a disagreement with someone, you still have to film with them the next day. In real life, if you have a fight with a friend, you can take a beat, think things through, cool off, and reach out when you're ready.

Not only do you have to see your castmates every day or so, but you have to talk about what went down and how you hate each other or how this one hates that one, which is then on camera for everyone to watch back when the show airs a few months later. In other words, nothing ever goes away, it gets played back and relived over and over again. Imagine if that happened every time you argued with your significant other or a close friend.

On the flip side, some incredible relationships are formed, also because these women spend a lot of time together and the conversations are often very passionate. People fight and make up. Then they fight again and make up again. It's ongoing and, to a certain degree, it's like marriage. In an ideal world, you're able to disagree, work through it, and love each other more afterward. For Kyle's part, she's become best friends with Teddi Mellencamp thanks to the show. She's also great friends with Dorit Kemsley.

Unfortunately, that doesn't always happen, as was the case with Lisa Vanderpump. At first, they were super tight. And then a lot of shit occurred on and off TV, and today they don't speak at all. They went from being amazing friends to avoiding each other in public. What it came down to is that Kyle felt Lisa was one of those people who always had to have her way, and everything was always about her. When things didn't go as Lisa liked, Kyle thought she just couldn't handle it. In Kyle's mind, Lisa needed to be the queen, and she definitely didn't appreciate being challenged by Kyle, who was absolutely going to call her out on her crap.

The fact is, it's never ideal to fall out with someone who's an important part of your life, but if making peace with them means changing who you are or hiding your honest feelings, sometimes there's nothing you can do about it. The good news is that you're typically better off for it in the long run. When someone shows you their true colors, you should always believe them.

THE HOUSE HUSBANDS

While the ladies are 100 percent the stars of *The Real Housewives* franchise, the husbands and significant others add that extra layer of entertainment to the show, and I've definitely formed some great bonds by being a part of it. Adrienne Maloof's ex, Paul Nassif, is still a good friend of mine. I actually just listed his house. Ken Todd, Lisa Vanderpump's husband, was a cool dude, and I enjoyed our time spent together. And, these days, I'm particularly close with Lisa Rinna's husband, Harry Hamlin, and Dorit Kemsley's husband PK. In fact, PK and I are looking at collaborating on a business venture.

One important thing about these guys is that I can share a lot of stuff with them that my friends who are not on the show don't necessarily get—everything from the actual experiences to the overall lifestyle. PK has also assisted me with some challenging business decisions.

But, ultimately, we're all there to support our partners no matter what. In my mind, Kyle is never wrong when it comes to being on the show. I remember when Dorit first joined the cast and PK said to me, "Can you please help me navigate this thing?" The first pieces of advice I gave him, which he reiterates to this day, were, "If you're going to speak up and have an opinion about something, make it real, make it interesting for television, then shut up and let the rest of the shit go down with the wives. And, *always* agree with your wife!"

FAMILY TIES

When family relationships meet reality television it's usually more complex than friendships, because—at the end of the day—these people are your actual relatives and resentments can run higher. Even the littlest disparities can be exacerbated into huge dramas.

Kyle has experienced this with both of her sisters—Kim and Kathy—who've been on separate seasons of the show with her. And it's not easy, to say the least. By nature, Kyle has a huge heart and is very protective of them, even though she's the baby in the family. She never wants there to be any negativity, especially because she loves her nieces so much—she really tries her best to keep the peace.

At the end of the day, that's all she can do. People are who they are, on and off the show. When there's that much love, what comes with it is a lot more tension and much higher stakes. My hope is that they'll always figure out a way to look past their differences and find their way back to each other, no matter what. That's what family is about.

TIMING IS EVERYTHING

Over the past fifteen years, I've been offered a lot of TV show opportunities, including *Million Dollar Listing*, concepts like *Selling Sunset*, projects for HGTV, and so on. I've always turned them down because I never wanted a show to be purely about me; I wanted it to be about the collaborative business I'm running.

I'd tried to do the kind of show I envisioned with Evolution Media, but it didn't work out. We pitched to Bravo and, at that time, they didn't want it. They felt like they had *Million Dollar Listing* and that there wasn't room for another real estate show on the network.

Then, five years ago, Justin Hochberg and Adam Sher from ITV called me and said, "We really want to pitch you an idea that we think will go far." I thought to myself, *Another show, whatever*. But I agreed to meet at my office and have a conversation. I figured I'd turn the tables and pitch them what I wanted to do.

So they came in, and Justin Hochberg was very funny. He walked into my office and said, "I know your time is valuable. I'm going to pitch you in two minutes, and in two minutes you're going to say yes."

I was like, "Okay!"

Then he put his iPad on the table, started a timer, and said, "I want to create a real estate show with you and here's the name." He turned his iPad around and there was my logo for The Agency.

Without hesitation, I said, "I'm in."

He laughed and replied, "I asked for two minutes, and I did it in one."

As I said, I've always wanted to create a show that's bigger than I am in the same way that I wanted to create a business that's bigger than I am. And I wanted it to be about The Agency. We have so many amazing people on our team, and there are so many unbelievable stories to tell.

Finally, Netflix came to us and the director, Unscripted Originals (the buyer for reality), Jenn Levy, was someone I'd worked with at Bravo, so she was already familiar with me. She said she wanted to buy the show, which was very exciting. Originally, they wanted to base it in Mexico, which meant it was going to be in Spanish, in part because I'm originally from there and we have multiple offices there, but also because they were looking for content for Latin America, where it's a lot less expensive to film.

In February 2020, I went to Mexico City and met with the production team, and we knew we'd be ready to start filming in March or April. Of course that was when COVID hit, which put the kibosh on our plans and delayed things for a while.

When the regulations for filming ended, they were still very challenging in Mexico, so the people at Netflix called me and said, "I know it's been a while now and we haven't done anything. We have bad news and hopefully good news. *The Agency Mexico* isn't going to happen. But we want to do a show called, *Buying Beverly Hills*, which will be centered around The Agency." I loved that idea!

So we did an internal open casting among our Los Angeles agents, which was roughly 450 of them at the time. We never looked outside of The Agency. Remarkably about eighty people threw their hats in the ring and went on tape for Netflix to consider. Then we narrowed it down again and again until we finally came to an agreement. At the end of the day, Netflix had final say, but I definitely had strong opinions too. There was one agent they didn't want to bring on, and I fought for him to be on the show. In the same vein, I also nixed two people whom I knew wouldn't be a good fit.

It's absolutely a Umansky family affair, as Netflix wanted it to be. My father and sister both make appearances, and my daughters Farrah and Alexia are the two main characters. I remember when I first told them about it. I asked them to take a ride with me to look at a new listing we had in Santa Barbara and I said, "I have some super exciting news. Netflix agreed to do *Buying Beverly Hills* instead of a show based in Mexico. It's going to be amazing for The Agency."

They asked me who was going to be part of the cast, and I laughed and replied, "Well, you two are going to be the stars. I already committed you!" They were like, *What?!* But of course they were also very excited and knew that it was really up to them. Both Farrah and Alexia were completely gung ho from that moment on.

We're all extremely proud of the first season of the show we created, which premiered on November 4, 2022, and included all the fabulous real estate porn, the multimillion-dollar transactions, and also the real-life stories of our agents. It offered an exclusive look into The Agency and the high-stakes world of ultra-luxury real estate. For the first time, viewers were able to watch me in the role of CEO and boss (not just as a loving father and husband as many have seen for years on *RHOBH*) and also the unique dynamic of working with my daughters and our top agents. It dug deep into our family interactions, both my actual family, and also the larger "family" of all of our employees and the difficulties and struggles that were inherent in that.

The most famous zip code in the entire world is 90210, and our goal was to showcase the incredible properties we represent and share what it takes to get them sold. It was the first time a home over $100 million was featured on a TV show.

We also wanted it to follow young professionals on their

journey, and provide real lessons and a reflection of what's required to succeed as an agent and at The Agency. We raised questions like: *Do the younger agents have what it takes to reach my level? Do they have what it takes to be at The Agency, and will they survive? What are their hurdles? How do I teach somebody to become a million dollar listing agent?*

What's really cool is that Netflix bought the franchise, which means that we'll likely branch out to *Buying London, Buying Miami,* and so on—similar to *The Real Housewives.* The possibilities are endless.

The message here is that, sometimes, even when an opportunity exists, it may not be the right opportunity for you. You have to believe in your instincts and trust that everything will happen when it's supposed to.

MAURICIO'S MANTRAS

- Once you've evaluated a situation and made a decision, don't second-guess it. If you're constantly doubting yourself, you can't deliver with excellence, because you'll always be taking two steps forward and one step back.

- When you're in the public spotlight, you have to separate your on-camera life from your real life and, even when people gossip about you, remain authentic.

- You have to be confident in who you are as a person and not change that for anyone.

- Fame can ruin friendships, and it can foster friendships; as long as you hold your head high, the people you can trust will rise to the top.

- When someone shows you their true colors, you should always believe them.

- Featuring family relationships on television can be very challenging, because—at the end of the day—they're your actual relatives, and resentments can run higher.

- If an opportunity doesn't feel right to you, no matter how much you want it, you have to walk away. Trust that everything will happen when it's supposed to.

CHAPTER 11

KEEP MOVING

If you can't fly, run; if you can't run, walk; if you
can't walk, crawl, but by all means keep moving.
—Martin Luther King Jr., civil rights leader

COMPETITION MAKES YOU STRONGER

What's so beautiful about free market competition is that not
only does it allow you to build a more robust company but it
also makes you more resilient as a human being. Let's face it,
every superhero needs a villain—someone who pushes you to
work harder and to strive to be better every single day. For The
Agency, our Goliath is a company called Compass. Six months
after we were born, they launched with similar ideologies,
namely to take the real estate industry—which was relatively
broken—and disrupt it. Their approach in doing this was going
to be through technology and by raising an enormous sum

of money with what we believed was the intent of creating a monopoly.

To give you a sense of what we were up against, they raised roughly $1.6 billion when they started their company. By comparison, we raised $1 million. But more to the point, their strategies seemed to us to be mean-spirited. We thought their goal was to corner the market share and become dominant by possibly raiding agents and offering commission compressions—which is when agents lower their commission for the same service they'd typically provide for a full commission. Unfortunately for them, since their tactics did not seem to me to be morally sound, the exact opposite happened.

I'll never forget one specific dinner many years ago when Robert Reffkin, the CEO of Compass, was talking to me about the company's plan to grow around the United States. Here's how I remember the conversation: I asked him, "How do you expect to continue buying all of the other firms and not have any competition? What's going to happen when clients' homes don't sell, they're unhappy, and they want to switch brokerages? How are you going to handle that?"

His response was "They're just going to change teams within Compass."

Surprised by his confidence in something that made no sense to me, I countered, "That's not the way a consumer understands behavior or the way consumers behave themselves. They're not going to blame the individual team but rather the larger brokerage. And, as a result, other brokerages will be born."

He shook his head in disbelief, so I added, "Your expectation is to create a monopoly."

He scoffed at that, responding, "We don't use that word."

I found this amusing because it was exactly the word I thought described his plan. Not only that, but I was thrilled to hear it, because I know that monopolistic experiences cannot successfully exist, which meant The Agency would be there to pick up the pieces when Compass imploded.

Going back about two years ago, an article published in the press stated that Compass—deemed our main opponent—was pilfering all of our agents, which was somewhat false. In general, I thought the piece was about 50 percent truth and 50 percent bullshit. But it didn't matter. It was out there in the universe, and people were reading it and believing it. Needless to say, that wasn't good publicity for us.

At that point, I had to ask myself what the most proactive course of action was. How should we react as a company? How can we create better employee retention during Compass's attack on our livelihood? How do we find more agents? Sure, we could have sat there and harped on the unfair slant of the article. We could have asked for a retraction or tried to retaliate. We also could have thrown in the towel. But, instead, we decided to take a step backward and reanalyze who we were and what led us to attain our current level of success. We didn't bite back. That would have fostered more negativity, which is not our style. We continued to live and preach what The Agency is all about—a culture of family, togetherness, and collaboration, which isn't necessarily for everyone. And our feeling is, and has always been, if you don't believe in our methodology, then you don't belong here. When you work at The Agency, you're going to be one of a smaller group that holds the flag. When you go to Compass, you're going to be one of thirty thousand. Which would you prefer?

So our first and most important step was to reach out to our people, those who'd been loyal to us, to make sure they knew how much we appreciated them and that they were an integral part of our team.

The second thing I did was befriend the writer of the article so I could demonstrate all of the amazing things The Agency was doing through complete transparency. We had nothing to hide, and I wanted that to be abundantly clear. I knew that if I could present a positive and authentic perspective on things, the next time this writer went to research a piece on real estate, the facts would be evident and the result would be more favorable toward us.

Ultimately, things did not materialize the way Compass expected, and they were not able to buy everyone else out. Why? Because we remained optimistic and made calculated moves to rise above their attacks. Revisiting the idea that business is a chess game—in this event—we pulled our pawns back and retreated. We stopped spending as much money, and our company became healthier because of that.

Right now we're very excited; we just finished a big money raise and we're looking at potentially going public sooner than later. Contrary to the way I believe they've grown, we've built our company responsibly and have been profitable every single year. We understand the brokerage model, which, in my opinion, Robert Reffkin does not.

Regardless, I've always enjoyed the competition with Compass. It drives me. Honestly, had they not done something so big and so extraordinary, I may have not been as motivated to want to be global. I may have been content with being strictly a Los Angeles brand.

Still, I'm watching Compass like a hawk. There's no question about it. They're undoubtedly our biggest challenger, except I think their tactics are irresponsible. I'd equate them to the dark side in Star Wars, whereas The Agency is the light side. They seem to rely on brute force while we're like the Little Engine That Could. We act ethically and rely on positive energy to generate progress.

We're not going after them guns blazing, and we're not going to stoop to any of what I view as their underhanded maneuvers; we concentrate on doing the right thing and negotiating profitable deals. Thanks to that practicality, we're coming out ahead. Right now I'm approaching a checkmate, which is very gratifying.

I believe The Compass *Titanic* will sink eventually. And when it does, I plan to have a bunch of lifeboats out there ready to save their best agents. Let the saga continue . . . for now.

EVERY DAY I'M HUSTLIN'

Even when it seems like you've achieved everything you want, you can always work harder, continue to hustle, and maintain a happy, balanced life.

One of my philosophies is to not look backward. Moving forward is really the only thing that we have in our lives. It's about continuing to push yourself and find new opportunities. From the very beginning, my partner Billy and I have always said, let's open a door and see what's on the other side. We never talked about limitations, because we firmly believed—and still do—that the possibilities are endless.

I remember one specific time, getting out of the shower (again, where I do most of my big thinking), and calling Billy to excitedly tell him, "I figured it out, we're going to create a global company and open up franchises all over the world."

He replied, "I don't know how you're going to do that, but I support you one hundred percent." And that's exactly what we're doing.

One of the reasons we've been so effective in our pursuit is that we're willing to make mistakes and to learn from those mistakes. We never get caught up in our current situation, especially if it doesn't feel right. The day you stop learning is the day you get bored, and the day you get bored is the day you stop driving forward and you stop being enthusiastic about what you're doing.

With that in mind, it's important to note that you can't say yes to every single prospect. There's a difference between considering the open door and walking through it. You have to take a beat to analyze whether the opportunity is in your best interest and, often, those decisions need to be made very quickly. Generally speaking, I rely on my gut feeling and that typically leads me down the correct path. Of course that gut feeling is based on the knowledge I've accrued and the many lessons I've learned throughout the years.

I do want to point out that things won't always go the way you expected or hoped they would. And that's okay. It then becomes a question of how you deal with it, how you keep pushing, and how you pivot.

In order to continue hustling and moving forward, The Agency recently made a major acquisition, which was featured prominently in the media. Here's an excerpt from *Real Estate Weekly*:

> Global real estate brokerage, The Agency today announced that they have acquired Triplemint, a revolutionary technology-powered, NYC-based firm,

in an all-equity transaction. The Agency will adopt Triplemint's proprietary, disruptive technology, and Triplemint will adopt The Agency's innovative, industry-leading brand. Going forward, the companies will jointly operate as The Agency. Together, the two are forming an agent-first, tech-driven boutique luxury global broker-age firm. In tandem with the acquisition, The Agency has jointly raised $35 million in growth capital from strategic investors, further positioning The Agency for strategic and sustainable global growth.

The Triplemint opportunity came about because the pres-ident of our company was on a panel with the CEO of Triple-mint and they were talking about philosophies and culture and the way they saw the business. By the end of the panel, they both realized how similar their views were and, also, that they each possessed unique strengths, so they decided to talk about working together. Shortly thereafter, we started to think about merging and creating something even bigger and better as a team.

Suddenly, I had to ask myself: *Am I willing to give up nearly half of my company in order to take this next huge step?* That was a massive decision, and I thought long and hard about whether one plus one was going to equal five or if it was only going to equal two, in which case it wouldn't have been worth it. Since

I believed the former to be the case, we went ahead with the deal, which ended up being slightly in our favor.

That being said, our work is far from done. Integrating two companies is extraordinarily challenging, but I know it will pay off in the long run.

And, in the meantime, we'll be hustling and pushing every day to make sure that happens. Anything short of that wouldn't be our style.

MAURICIO'S MANTRAS

- Don't let competition sidetrack you. Instead, use it to your advantage to build a stronger company and become a more resilient human being.

- Business is a chess game; sometimes you have to pull your pawns back and retreat in order to come out ahead.

- Even when it seems like you've reached the pinnacle of your career, you can always work harder, continue to hustle, and maintain a happy, balanced life.

- Never look backward. Moving forward is really the only thing we have in our lives. It's about continuing to push yourself and find new opportunities. You have to open every door and see what's on the other side. When you do that, the possibilities are endless.

- The day you stop learning is the day you get bored, and the day you get bored is the day you stop driving forward and you stop being enthusiastic about what you're doing.

- You can't say yes to every single prospect. There's a difference between considering the open door and walking through it. You have to take a beat to analyze whether the opportunity is in your best interest.

- Things won't always go the way you expected or hoped they would. And that's okay. It then becomes a question of how you deal with it, how you keep pushing, and how you pivot.

THE FUTURE IS BRIGHT

I have no plans of slowing down any time soon. The future is bright, and the trajectory for both my career and Kyle's continues to trend upward. We have very high aspirations and are willing to invest the time, the energy, and the passion it takes to keep growing.

Kyle is enjoying acting more than anything, and she's also in the midst of writing a couple of shows that she'll produce. I expect a few years from now she'll step away from being in front of the camera and do a lot more creating and producing.

From my perspective, as far as building The Agency, we're looking to create an even bigger global real estate brand. We'd like to be everywhere, so we're raising a lot of money and putting in a substantial amount of capital for the first time in order to make that happen.

I believe we're at the perfect point now where we're well-known enough—with multiple offices in California, numerous locations across the United States and in Mexico and Canada, and one each in Turks and Caicos, Cayman Islands, and Amsterdam—and ready to continue to expand worldwide. My dream is to one day get off my yacht at the marina in Saint-Tropez and run into an Agency office, and then fly to Capri on my private plane and stop into another Agency location. As I said in the last chapter, my ultimate goal is to take the company public, which I believe is absolutely achievable, and to finally have developed a large-scale, universally recognized, international brand that started in my head.

On the personal front, nothing is more important to me than my family.

What I look forward to the most is quality time with Kyle and my kids and watching my four daughters continue to succeed and possess the same passion for life that I do.

My journey hasn't always been easy, and it definitely hasn't been boring. It's been unpredictable, exhilarating, and emotionally and physically demanding at times. And I've cherished every minute of it. The knowledge I've absorbed through my many experiences has been priceless, and my purpose in writing this book was to communicate that knowledge, along with the strategies I've taught myself, to anyone and everyone looking to build their own fruitful career and to find the happiness we all seek in life.

THE AGENCY RULE BOOK

The Agency was founded for real estate agents by real estate agents who aspired to progress and modernize the industry. We set out to foster a culture of partnership, where agents could share their knowledge and spheres of influence. Basically, we threw out the rule book and created our own. Essentially, we make our own rules . . . and then we break them. *That's just our style.*

RULE #1: NO ASSHOLES

We choose character and culture over suits and ties.

Mauricio's Mantra: It's extremely important to maintain an environment of professional collaboration that makes your employees feel good.

RULE #2: HAVE FUN

We have a unique perspective on the world that drives our business, fuels innovation, and fosters creativity.

Mauricio's Mantra: Since work is where people spend most of their waking hours, there should always be an element of fun—this will help foster productivity.

RULE #3: STAY HUNGRY

We began as disruptors, and disruptors we shall remain.

Mauricio's Mantra: In order to be truly successful, you should never be satisfied with what you've accomplished; you should always want more. For example, don't take your commission and go on a vacation. Instead, think about your next steps.

RULE #4: ALL FOR ONE AND ONE FOR ALL

When you work with one of us, you work with all of us.

Mauricio's Mantra: Traditionally speaking, the real estate industry is considered a very cutthroat business, where people hide their contacts, their deals, and their inventory. A better approach is to view your company as one big family. You all rise and celebrate together, and, when the going gets tough, you all suffer and fall together.

RULE #5: WE'RE HERE TO SERVE

Anticipating needs and going the extra mile is just our standard.

Mauricio's Mantra: Always remember that customer service is king. Catering to clients is your job. Great hospitality and attention to detail wins every time.

RULE #6: MAKE SOME NOISE

We've elected to stand apart, be ourselves, have our voices heard.

Mauricio's Mantra: In order to make sure you're heard in the market, you have to be loud. You want to be part of your community and make sure the people in it know that you're there through the good and the bad.

RULE #7: TELL IT LIKE IT IS

We make the headlines black, white, and read all over. And leave them wanting more.

Mauricio's Mantra: Don't lie, don't pretend, don't exaggerate; just be direct. Clients will always appreciate that.

RULE #8: MORE OF THE SAME IS NEVER AN OPTION

Because following the crowd will take you no further than the crowd.

Mauricio's Mantra: Innovate, take risks, and never be complacent with what you're doing.

RULE #9: DARE TO DREAM

We seek out like-minded rebels, who embrace our core standards of integrity, collaboration, and creativity.

Mauricio's Mantra: Give your employees the confidence to dream, to create, and to think outside the box. It's not okay to do things a certain way just because that's how you've been doing it for years. Change is necessary in order to achieve progress.

RULE #10: RULES WERE MEANT TO BE BROKEN

Except No Assholes. We're firm on that one.

Mauricio's Mantra: It's okay to break the rules, even your own, when it makes sense. But showing up with a negative attitude is out of the question.

ACKNOWLEDGMENTS

With all the stories I share in this book, none of them would be complete without acknowledging the people in my life who have shared in my journey and supported me.

To Kyle, the heartbeat of my life and our family. Nothing would be possible without your unconditional love and support. Writing this book brought back so many memories and you were with me every step of the way. Thank you for being my biggest cheerleader. I love you.

To my girls, Farrah, Alexia, Sophia, and Portia, you are the reason I strive to be better every day. My relationship with each of you is my greatest accomplishment, and it is my joy to watch your lives unfold.

To my parents, Eduardo and Estella, and sister, Sharon, your love made me who I am today. All that I've learned from you has been instrumental in shaping how I raise my family and run my business. I am proud that we get to continue working together with the next generation of our family.

To The Agency family, whether you've been there since

day one or just joined us, your individual story is what motivates me when I think about the future of our company. I am honored to work alongside the hardest-working and most dedicated people in the business.

To Billy Rose, thank you all for your trust and for your willingness to go on this journey with me. I am amazed by what we have accomplished in eleven years and look forward to all that is in store for us in the future.

To Blair Chang, Paul Lester, Aileen Comora, and Santiago Arana, who stepped up to make the dream of The Agency and its growth a reality. Thank you for your wisdom and friendship over the years. This story of The Agency is as much mine as it is yours.

To George Santopietro and Glenn Spiro, I'm eternally grateful for all that I've learned from you.

To Jen Bergstrom, thank you for giving me this opportunity. Thank you to the team at Simon & Schuster for making this book possible: Natasha Simons, Caroline Pallotta, Sally Marvin, Mia Robertson, Lauren Truskowski, Bianca Ducasse, Samantha Hoback, and Jaime Putorti. To Emily Liebert, thank you for bringing my memories and thoughts to life.

To Alyssa Reuben and WME, thank you for taking great care of me.

To my right hand who's been with me for years, Jane, I can't do much without you.

To everyone who has shared their own stories of entrepreneurship and growth with me over the years, thank you. Keep pushing and keep learning.